Life in the Balance

David Crabb

Life in the balance

First Edition 2002
Second Edition 2020

Copyright © 2002 David Crabb

Photograph of HMS Fife Crown copyright used with permission

Photographs of HMS Galatea/Cod war incidents taken by ships photographer, used with permission

All other Photographs authors private collection

All scripture references taken from Zondervan NIV study bible basic library

Quotes by Winston Churchill taken from "Winston Churchill quotations" Jarrold publishing

Any unidentified 'quotes' from remembered sermons, acknowledgement is given, and apologies for not being able to recall specific details

Life in the balance

Dedication and Acknowledgements

I dedicate this book to my wife Sheila, who has been my constant companion, as together we have discovered the God of the way through. Her love, dedication, and wonderful ability to always see the best in me, have helped immensely in keeping me on the road of continual growth. Her example in faith and her strength of character have often been the anchors that have kept me steady, as I have often floundered when daring to step out upon the waters once again.

Life in the balance

In Memory of my parents

Bert & Betty Crabb

Life in the balance

About the author

David was Senior Pastor of the growing Elim church in Rugby, and ministered there for 21 years. They went on to pastor a church in Croydon for a further seven years. Married, to Sheila since 1977, they have two children and seven grandchildren.

From the age of 15, David spent nine years in the Royal Navy, becoming a Christian at the age of 29. Almost immediately it was evident there was a call upon his life, and he began studying the word of God. After two years of various correspondence studies he began a foundational course at Elim Bible College, Capel, graduating in 1987 and beginning full-time ministry in the same year.

Postgraduate studies continued, and David was accepted for ordination into the Elim ministry in 1991. Serving since 1987 as the assistant pastor, David and Sheila took over the ministry in Rugby in January 1990.

David has additionally trained in Counselling, Pastoral Supervision, Life Coaching and gained a Post Grad certificate in Missional Leadership. He has been a Regional Trainer for Pastoral Care UK; serving also on the board of the Association of Christian Counsellors. He is now serving as Deputy Centre Manager of the Teen Challenge Centre Willoughby House.

Life in the balance

Introduction

My walk with God began with great passion and a real desire to prove my devotion to Jesus. I thought I would go to any length to show my love for Him. This love and devotion always true. However, I have learnt, and continue to learn, that at times it can almost give out or even give in. This has nearly always been due to the ignorance in my heart concerning myself.

There have been times in my life when, because I did not know how to go on, I have been tempted to run away. A little like the disciples at Gethsemane, almost certainly they didn't want to run, but their souls had not developed sufficiently for them to stand their ground. There are times when the Lord allows crisis in our lives to reveal our hearts to us, and to create within us a greater desire for more of His tangible presence. So often we live with a belief that we do not need to continually receive the Holy Spirit, until we discover afresh how spiritually poor we have been, or are in danger of becoming.

Some, while enduring a 'sifting process,' have this revealed to them by transgressing some kind of moral boundary. Simon Peter experienced this when he denied Jesus. This is not God's ideal way for us to grow. However, it would seem that there are times that we almost need to be forced into growth. Either willingly or forcibly, He will take us through the dark night of our soul.

God has shown me that indeed His desire is to bless me; however, my idea of blessing and His can often be very different. I have discovered that God is actually willing to allow any lesser dreams I may have to be shaken away. For

Life in the balance

His desire as Larry Crabb reveals in his excellent book "Shattered dreams" is to meet with us.

This book is about pilgrimage. If you are looking for seven easy steps, or five golden principles, this book is not for you. However, if like me, you have discovered that there are roads that we find ourselves on, that lead us through all kinds of experiences, leaving indelible marks upon our lives and even at times bringing moments of incredible pain, confusion and can I say embarrassment, then like me, you have realised our God is the God of the 'way through.'

He simply will not let us off the hook. I have fought at times tooth and nail; I have manipulated, I have run away, I have done all manner of things in order to try and discover the way round, the way out, even, at times, the way back. Well, there are times in our lives (usually more than one) when we learn just how insistent our God can be.

During these times of 'growth,' when it can seem as though everything is in the balance, I have often done what many Christians do, that is to don the countenance of the good martyr who suffers for the Lord without complaining, (except on the inside). However, there are times I wonder about God! Does He really care? Why is it that during my worst moments He seems so far away? All I need during thoughts like that is for someone to come up to me, and say, "Cheer up! It hurts me more than it hurts you." At times I found that as hard to believe as my dad, who, like many dads before him assures the unfortunate recipient that the impending punishment is going to cause 'them personally' so much discomfort.

In fact, our heavenly Father does discipline those He loves. I used to find that scripture easy to believe, the concept was obvious, I could understand the need for Him to be 'Fatherly' in that way, just as I was to my own kids. Of course, it was

Life in the balance

still easy to believe in my early adolescent years as a Christian, and even during my early years in ministry. God always seemed to back me! I almost felt like King Midas, everything I touched turned to gold. My lessons then were far less painful (or so it seems, I have a feeling David Crabb then would have contested that view).

During the first few months of my conversion I was given a song that has been for me almost like a prophetic word from God – I call it *"The Portrait Song."* Along with it I was given the scripture Isaiah 35. I received it as a promise, and I leave the words to the song with you now in the hope that you will find Him to be the absolutely faithful God that I have and still am discovering Him to be. No matter what I have thrown back at him in my frustration, pain and at times sheer anger, He has continued His wonderful work, patiently leading me, at times I am sure fencing me in, protecting me when I am not even aware, allowing me to undergo unpleasant experiences that although hurt, teach me so much.

I encourage you, don't give in; keep hold of him even during your desperation, especially when you feel as though you are in the balance. He is the God of the way through, and He will take you through if you will let Him.

Life in the balance

The Portrait song

I'm your Father, don't you know?
Fathers love their children so,
It hurts me when you walk away at the start of every day.
Then when you're hurt you wonder why,
You turn to me and you start to cry,
You even think I might not care can't you see I'm always there.
So turn around my precious son come walk with me for I'm the one,
Who loves you more than you could know,
Come walk with me and I will show you love, true love, my love.

Inside I see you hate yourself,
You're feeling like you're on the shelf,
You often seek to find a fault but I'm the one who made the mould.
You cannot change the kind of man,
I've made you for I hold the plan,
But trust in me and lift your heart I saw the end before the start.
So, look again and understand just who I modelled for my plan,
The spirit you now have inside was dearly bought that's why I died for you,
I died for you.

So, I say to you give up the fight,
For it's not by power or by might,
But by my spirit you will be the son creation waits to see.
For you're the picture I will paint,
A masterpiece without a taint,
For every good work takes its time but I'll finish it for you are mine.
I've painted many others too, but don't compare for who are you?
To pull apart or criticise, for all my pictures are beautiful in my eyes,
In my eyes, in my eyes.

Time is what I say will be,
The end of all is up to me,
But this I say remember well,
My pictures I will never sell,
I have a home for you to be a place that lasts eternally,
And there I'll keep you close to me the artist and his gallery.
So no more worries no more cares,
Just try to keep away from snares,
Don't listen to the devils lies he'll try to rob you of your prize in me,
Your homes with me, come to me, my master piece.

Life in the balance

Contents

Portrait song

Introduction
Chapter one   The Secret
Chapter one   Runaway
Chapter two   Pressure
Chapter three   Pressing on through pressure
Chapter four   Facing the past
Chapter five   Frozen in the storm
Chapter six   The Desert of no short cuts
Chapter seven   Quiet waters
Chapter eight   Beware the polluted holes
Chapter nine   Don't Wail, Travail
Chapter ten   A Fathers faith
Chapter eleven   Weighing up
Chapter twelve   The Way Through
Chapter thirteen   He has nothing in me
Chapter fourteen   Anchors away, all ahead full
Chapter fifteen   In the wake
Epilogue

Life in the balance

Chapter One - The Secret

I guess we could all be described, to varying degrees, as 'damaged goods.' I mean we all have our secrets, don't we? David Shearman senior pastor at the Talbot Street church in Nottingham once said, "I'm damaged goods, I am in recovery and I have learnt some stuff."

We all wear masks to cover up, hide behind, or perhaps present an image that is not entirely complete or true. Lurking beneath the mask is fear, fear of rejection. Fear that if we were fully known we would be found at the least wanting. For some it is enough to try and come to terms with yourself, let alone learn to be loved and accepted by others. Simply put we are all 'cracked pots,' some may conclude 'crack pots.'

In producing this second edition of Life in the Balance I was asked if I would be willing to include more detail of my own pilgrimage. It would seem that many have been able to connect with some of my own experiences and many of the experiences I have shared with my wife Sheila. Of course, I am happy to share details of my life, (most of them), but my belief is that there are no answers in the past. It is necessary to 'understand' your own life's experiences, to know where you have come from. However, as one who has travelled now a number of deep valleys I am utterly convinced that it has never been our Father's intention that valleys are for remaining in. Valleys are for 'passing through' and as we pass through we grow. It is finding the 'way' that can often prove to be difficult, so as an 'under shepherd' I hope and pray that my story may bring some 'sign posts' for some, maybe even the occasional water hole for others to draw refreshment from.

Life in the balance

So why begin this second edition with a chapter on secrets? Well, it is my opinion that it is the 'secret things' in our lives that often cause us the most pain. We all carry things. I have come across many now who have carried things into their ministries only to discover that in fact those things, if not dealt with, can become the very things that are the main factors in taking them out of ministry. Sadly, it would seem that many have the view that to be a 'poser' is necessary for a successful ministry and therefore the secrets are never dealt with.

We are very complicated creatures. Added to our complexity are the ravages that sin has had upon our characters and our personalities. Character of course refers to that which we are when we are alone, who we are in the dark when no one else is around. Personality ought to be a simple manifestation of that which is within, however if we are honest that is rarely the case in a complete sense....

My earliest memories are of a happy, contented little boy who found much pleasure in the very simplest of things. Treasured memories of riding around on a tiny tricycle, up and down a little back lane at the rear of our home. Other times I could be found pulling a large toy London bus up and down the avenue on the end of an old piece of string. I had a very active imagination, more than happy with my own company, keeping myself amused for hours on end playing games, making up stories and adventures in which I was the hero.

Our home in those days was generally happy. We lived in a three bedroomed, mid terrace house, in a pretty part of the town called Hillmorton. At that time there was Mum and Dad, my older sister Rosemary who shared a bedroom with my grandmother, who also lived with us. I had the little box room at the front of the house. I was to later share this with my

Life in the balance

brother Nigel who was born in 1960. My favourite memories of that house are always concerning Christmas time. At that time of year access was allowed into the front room, in the late fifties and early sixties most families had a 'posh room.' Dad would call us after all the preparations had been completed to come down stairs in order that we might open our presents. We were so fortunate; there were always two huge piles of presents for Rose and I to open. The presents would continue to come all day for there were so many visitors throughout the day and at the huge party that we would have in the evening. Mum and Dad had numerous friends, many of them through a band dad was part of called 'The Avalons.'

At that time a large part of our lives was spent at a local social club. I have many happy memories of that club; we looked forward to our Saturday nights there. The bags of crisps with the little blue bags of salt, the Sunpat raisins and salted peanuts. My favourite tipple was either dandelion and burdock or strawberry cream soda. The serious part of the evening was when the 'bingo' was on, all the children had to sit down and be quiet at that point. On one occasion dad was called before the committee because of the unruly behaviour of his kids during the bingo! I recall making the mistake of getting my fingers trapped in a door when the bingo was on, how I howled! Then the entertainment would begin and once everyone had had plenty to drink the 'Cockles and Mussels man' would arrive.

My favourite time was when some of the older members began to tell their stories of the war years. If you sat patiently and endured their tales you were almost guaranteed a pat on the head and a few coins for your pocket, these were nearly always invested into more crisps or raisins. There are so many happy memories that I have of those early days, but there are also 'secrets.'

Life in the balance

One of those secrets is so buried within my sub-conscious that it has only been evidenced through flash back experiences that I have known over the years. I have concluded that God has not allowed me too much conscious memory of that for a reason. However, there are memories that I have had to come to terms with, to forgive others and myself for the consequences they were to have throughout my younger years.

A number of things took place, at more or less the same time in my life, that were to have 'devastating' effects upon me. Sexual abuse, bullying and fears of all kinds came into my life at a time when a child needs love, encouragement, and attention of a positive kind.

My parents were also going through difficult periods that often resulted in terrible arguments involving not only my parents but my grandmother as well. Looking back as an adult I can smile at the almost comic scenario that was often the result. On one occasion I recall my grandmother on her knees with her head in the gas oven declaring aloud that, *"I'm not long for this world."* My dad casually walked by and turned the oven on saying, *"You're not now."* On another occasion I recall an incident between by dad and my grandmother that ended up with dad wrapping an indoor tv aerial around her neck. One of the worst times was seeing my dad's suitcases by the back door, incidents like these created a terrible insecurity within me.

Dad was my hero! To me as a small boy he was indestructible. His stories of his times in the Navy thrilled me, he would have us all laughing until we were in tears as he related his exploits, I so wanted to be like him. I wanted to be tough, to be able to give any who crossed me a 'good hiding.' But in my eyes, I was already weak. Things were happening to me that I could not stop. I knew that somehow, they were wrong but there was nothing I could do. I dare not tell anyone, least of all my father

Life in the balance

I had already been programmed to believe it was my fault anyway. In fact, I actually believed that if I refused to do what I was told to do my abuser would tell my dad what I had done.

I became quite a morose little boy. Although I was able to have friendships at school I was never at ease being real with anyone. Because I was very small for my age I was often the subject of bullying and on those occasions, I would come home in tears I could see the disappointment in my father's eyes. On occasions I would be disciplined for not sticking up for myself. I was an uninitiated, unvalidated boy and very unhappy inside.

Once I did stick up for myself resulting in my bully losing his toe nail, due to the fact I dropped a brick on his foot and hit him in the eye with a stick causing a nasty cut, I was again disciplined. I really thought dad would be pleased with me.

Eventually, due to the fact that our family was growing (two sisters and two brothers, mum lost four children), we had to move to a larger home. This meant moving to a rougher area and a much older home that needed a lot of work doing to it. Obviously, this brought a lot more pressure onto my parents who were both working full time.

These were harder times; I now had another sister, Debbie and a younger brother Timothy and we all wanted attention. Fortunately, the move meant that my abuser did not have the access to me he had before, however on the odd occasion he found a way to get to me. The anger I felt was all internalised so that at a very young age I had already learnt how to hate myself.

This resulted in me trying so hard to be someone else. I would crave attention doing all kinds of things to get it. As I grew and developed I became extremely fit, being in the school

Life in the balance

cross-country team and the gymnastics team. I would constantly show off in order to receive the kind of attention I wanted. I could do all the moves that the famous 'muscle man' on 'Hughie Greens Opportunity Knocks' did. During parties at mum and dad's I would invariably be called in to perform. I loved these times for it gave me opportunity to present a persona that even I grew to like. But I knew it wasn't real.

Secrets have the effect of creating fear and fear has creative power. Fear creates all kinds of things; in my case I feared exposure, rejection and abandonment.

My last school photograph, taken a few short months before leaving home, to join the Royal Navy on February 15th 1971.

Life in the balance

Part One Chapter One - Runaway

I cannot be certain when this tendency to run away began, or indeed why. All I know is that it began when I was very young. I suspect it had something to do with fear, rooted in a conglomeration of insecurities and attempts to draw attention to myself. My first experience was quite successful. Having spent the whole day and most of the evening away, and having consumed my bag of "blackjacks" I decided to give myself up. The attention I received from my parents was well worth all the effort, so I decided to do it again. The thrashing I received after that attempt put, I thought, any further ideas to rest once and for all.

I recall a conversation with my father soon after my first 'runaway' experience. He said to me, "Son you cannot run away from life, life will always catch up with you." It's strange how some conversations remain with you.

My next experience wasn't to happen for some years, and in fact, it came at a time when even I was not expecting it. At the age of fifteen I had reached a time in my life when I was quite confident and hopeful about the future. My father had caught me giving my Grandmother, who lived with us, some 'lip,' and as a result I received a clout around the back of my head. For some reason I just snapped, I leapt up from the sofa (not something I usually did as a teenager) and raised my fists to my dad. I didn't even see the next blow coming. I did however, feel it. Lying on the carpet I noticed my father's fists were still tightly balled so I felt it better to remain where I was for the time being.

The Plan – It seemed to be a fantastic idea! There was a

Life in the balance

Coupon in the Daily Mirror, "Join the Navy, and see the world!" If I were to leave various leaflets and coupons around the house mum and dad would see them and of course immediately repent, begging me not to leave.

The reality – Dad was thrilled that I wanted to follow in his footsteps (I forgot he served for 15 years in the Royal Navy). This was not what was supposed to happen. Within two short months, at the tender age of fifteen (and a half), I was in.

I was very proud of the fact that I had passed, with flying colours my first exam, the Naval aptitude test. I was given a piece of paper with pictures of various tools; the question was a real poser. "Which of these tools would you use to tighten the wheel nut of a car?" Judging by the smirk on the chief Petty Officers face, someone must have put, "the screwdriver" no, it wasn't me.

The medical was quite an experience. It was very clear that the Royal Navy at that time were being very thorough, and the standard of men they were seeking was to be of a calibre that only young men like myself would fulfil. The medical took all of 30 minutes, involving several of us lined up, clothes off, one by one going through a series of short tests. It was quite humiliating; particularly as a young wren rating kept coming in and out of the room with various pieces of paper. She could not hide the smirk on her face as we were just stood there looking, to say the least, somewhat vulnerable.

The headmaster of my school was not happy about the situation, as I was supposed to be taking my CSE examinations. I was personally thrilled that, that was one experience I would now be missing out on. I never really enjoyed school, I now realise it was not that I could not achieve; I was just lazy and lacked any real motivation. Even when I was a toddler on taking me to a doctor, convinced I had

Life in the balance

'rickets' (a disease, children were susceptible to, caused by a vitamin D deficiency, leading to a softening of the bones), my mum and dad were informed that I was just, "bone idle." I was to discover on joining the Navy that if I wanted to advance myself, it would only be achieved through taking examinations. I learnt very quickly to be more motivated.

February 15th 1971 (decimal day) I stood on the platform at Birmingham New street station to catch the 'Cornishman' down to Plymouth, to join HMS Raleigh, the training establishment. The whole joining up procedure had taken less than two months. Dad decided this would be a good time to tell me about the facts of life, he muttered something about 'strange people' and to be careful, and that was that. To be honest, I hadn't a clue what he was going on about, it was still all so very unreal. I was excited, this was an adventure and I was basking still from the attention I had been receiving. A sumptuous meal, at a very expensive restaurant the evening before, now both mum and dad in tears waving me goodbye (I just new they would be sorry), finally my plan was working!

Sitting in the smoke-filled compartment with three other hopefuls I decided to inspect the contents of the carrier bag mum had packed for me. Sandwiches, of course, some crisps, a selection of confectionary for my sweet tooth, and a carton of Kiaora orange juice, Oh, And my 'DC Superman comic.' The only other things I was required to take were some toiletries, a clothes brush, shoe cleaning kit, and a few items of clothing, this was all contained in a "good food costs less at Sainsbury's paper carrier bag."

Somehow, I felt as though I did not fit in with my compatriots. They had cigarettes, beer, and a couple of editions of *playboy*. They didn't even notice me, they must have been in their mid to late twenties, and I was just fifteen (and a half) and had nothing they could ever want.

Life in the balance

Another plan – The feelings of adventure and victory over my parents were vanishing very quickly. I was now alone, responsible only to myself, and I needed friends. I was also dying to have a look at one of those magazines. I decided to go to the buffet car and bought my very first pack of cigarettes, (20 Extra), telling the counter staff they were for my dad. On my return I offered them around and was quickly accepted and found worthy of speaking to, (I still couldn't get hold of that magazine though). But success, I did get my first bottle of beer. I also got almost nine years for my 'running away' on this occasion in Her Majesty's Royal Navy. Like most plans that seem good at the time, this one backfired.

It didn't take too long for the plan to begin to show signs of unexpected difficulties. The wakeup call came when we arrived at Plymouth station. There was a lot of shouting and swearing, and several petty officers were marching around barking out orders. We were very quickly bundled on to the back of a naval wagon, and taken to the Torpoint Ferry where we crossed over to Torpoint, where the training establishment was situated.

The memory of standing on the ferry, listening to the chain clanking as we were pulled slowly to the other side remains with me. I had all kinds of misgivings, wondering what on earth I had got myself into. It was nothing like I had read in the glossy brochure. Everyone on that brochure was smiling, and they were all so friendly looking. The officers in the brochure were all looking benevolently at the guys who were either playing chess, or at a snooker table. Up to now not one of these officers had spoken to me as a human being; in fact, they spoke with a kind of contempt in their voices.

I also recall the incredible feelings of excitement as I saw for real my first Naval warships. HMS Eagle (an old aircraft

Life in the balance

carrier) lay at anchor waiting to be broken up having been decommissioned. There were many other vessels, I noted their armament, which meant little to me at the time. However, to a young 15-year old they were totally cool. Guns, missile systems, flags flapping in the breeze, the whole picture acted as a stimulus, and helped keep the feelings of cultural shock at bay. My first glimpse of real sailors, as a frigate made its way out of harbour. Ratings stood to attention in their bell-bottom trousers. Yes! I had made the right decision I was sure.

For some strange reason, on arrival at the base, one of the very first things we were given was a haircut. I had already had a short back and sides. I could not believe that the naval barber would get any more off but bless him, he did. I found it quite amusing when some of the more 'Hippy' types arrived at the barber's. It was clear that the barber really enjoyed his job, as their curly locks fell to the floor, and the looks of horror as all that was left was a little bit 'on top.' We were introduced to our class petty officer who seemed a nice chap, he genuinely seemed to realise that we were all still in shock, and our first day was fairly easy, with a trip to the Naafi in the evening.

However, the feelings of isolation got gradually worse, as I realised that there was a postal strike on, and therefore I could not even send a letter, and my parents were not on the telephone then. That seems strange in our world of mobile everything. However, my dad somehow managed to get a letter to me through the local careers office and their own mail delivery system. I can remember vividly the tears cascading down my face as I read that letter. My parents seemed almost an eternity away. One line remains with me even to this day, "keep your chin up son, I know it seems hard now, remember we love you." I think that was the first time I ever heard either of my parents communicate to me that I was loved.

Life in the balance

I felt totally cut off, and I am convinced that my boyhood ended that day. For most of that time I was very unhappy. I felt robbed of some very important years, and I constantly experienced homesickness. The cruellest part of it all was that because I joined at fifteen, at any time during those three years until I reached my 18th birthday, I could have left, as those years were classed as boy's service. Of course, I was either not made aware of that, or I simply did not understand that was the case.

At any rate, I was awaiting a call from either mum or dad begging me to come home. That call never came. So, in pride, I had to maintain the façade. Each time I came home on leave in my uniform, I again had the experience of being the centre of attention. I put on a mask that basically told everyone how much I loved Naval life, and the freedom of being my own man. I didn't need anyone.

On returning back to my base after a few days leave, I would be found at the back of the NAAFI building crying my eyes out. Or sitting in a lonely bar, listening to depressing records on the juke box, fooling no one, not even myself. I had decided to start smoking as I was convinced this was not only cool, but felt it made me look tough. I also started to drink a little, my favourite tipple then being 'brown ale.' I would go to the bar and with as deep a voice as possible, order a bottle of Newcastle brown or the like. Most times I was served out of sheer pity I'm sure.

I almost blew it in the early weeks. I was just returning to my barracks after another lonely evening in the NAAFI listening to a particular record, which was a favourite of my mums, (which shall remain nameless as I will never live it down).

I was shuffling along with my hands in my pockets (we were supposed to march everywhere), It was a dark, dirty, foggy

Life in the balance

night, and my mood was very similar. Suddenly someone shouted, "you boy, don't you know that it is customary to salute a naval officer." I responded, "I'm sorry sir, I didn't see you." To this day I will never forget his words, "Switch on your night vision lad." My hand moved slowly and deliberately to the side of my head, I was about to do what he had told me to. I was going to go click, click and switch on my night vision. But I chickened out and chopped him off a smart salute. He simply smirked and said, "Carry on lad, and wake up." That memory for some reason remained with me for many years. Though it was certainly expedient that I obeyed that officer, something within me had wanted to speak out, to stand up for myself, but it was crushed, as in the future it would often be. I was so angry because what he had said seemed to be so inane, and therefore merely a means of exercising his superior rank.

Another thing that made me very insecure was the realisation that in the Navy all the things that I had taken for granted would now be at the discretion of another. If I wanted leave for instance, I would have to fill in a request form, and that request could be denied, and sometimes was. Strangely enough this gave me real problems whilst at Bible College in Capel, as we were required to fill in forms when going home for the weekend, purely for catering purposes. I failed to realise that at first and became angry at the thought that someone may seek to interfere with my liberty as I saw it.

Well, my pride would not allow me to go back on my decision to join the Navy. Unlike my brother who a few years later also joined up, but after a few weeks found it was not for him. He left, and though he felt as though he had not managed to succeed is now a successful businessman, owning his own company, and I am pleased to say following the Lord. I should have got the message then. My brother simply said to my dad, "Don't worry dad, I'm not going to be a layabout."

Life in the balance

Dad was not disappointed in him at all, and he would not have been with me either, had I the courage to do what my heart so desperately wanted. But, unfortunately, I was going to have to learn the hard way. And hard it was.

The verbal and at times physical abuse was to a 15-year old simply terrifying. The regime was, it would seem, designed to break you. I recall on one occasion that our class petty officer thought it would be good to wake us all up at 2.00 am and give us a matter of minutes to pack all our kit up into our kit bag, and one suitcase. We were then ordered to double march up and down the road outside our accommodation block for 30 minutes, before unpacking again and returning to bed until 6.00am.

Some of the worst abuse occurred on the parade ground when doing drill. Hour after hour of constant verbal, and sometimes physical abuse, designed to break you, humiliate you and prepare you for the building up part of the course which came a few weeks later. I saw much older lads than me sitting in the corner sobbing with hurt, anger and utter frustration. Our own class leader had his 21st birthday during training. On hearing this, the parade drill instructor thought he would give him a present. He was ordered to run around the parade ground (which was very large) 21 times with a rifle above his head. He collapsed after about six circuits and hit his nose on falling over. He was required to clean the area of blood afterwards, and also required to apologise to the GI (gunnery instructor).

It seems inconceivable now that this kind of abuse would be tolerated, but things were very different then. We lost quite a few in the first couple of weeks, as things got harder and harder. I was fortunate, because at fifteen I was physically very fit. I used to be a cross-country runner and was also in the school gymnastics team. However, the only running I wanted to do then was to run away.

Life in the balance

Yet, amid all of this, there were times when I stood upon the parade ground in full uniform, and watched as the White Ensign was gracefully hoisted to the strains of "A life on the ocean wave," or "Hearts of Oak" even on one occasion, "all the nice girls love a sailor" like my compatriots, feelings of incredible pride, and a sense of being someone would fill my heart.

I remember my very first entry into a foreign port on HMS Fife, as we gracefully entered the harbour, stood to attention on the flag deck, a solitary piper stood on top of the bridge playing "Amazing Grace." Tears of pride cascaded down my face; at times like that I would wonder why I ever had doubts about the life I had embarked upon. And of course, there was no doubt that the uniform then had a remarkable effect, especially on the opposite sex.

I recall the occasion I had to report to have my first identity card photograph taken. The Naval photographer commented on how unhappy I looked, and tried his best to get me to try the faint glimmer of a smile. It was to no avail, as I am sure you will agree, and my face gave away my true feelings. On one occasion I even visited a naval chaplain, but to be honest I had no idea what he was waffling on about. He was talking about 'insecurities' and I really had no concept of what he was saying. I needed something a little more basic that would communicate hope to me, for in truth I had lost all hope, and already my young life was fast spiralling out of control.

Life in the balance

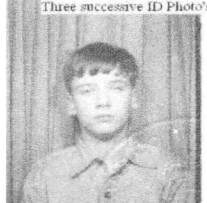

Three successive identity card photo's.

Top. 1971, on first joining up, and just before my second haircut, still in total shock and very unhappy. I simply refused to smile.

Middle. This one was taken about 1973 (still miserable) and well on the road of alcohol abuse.

The bottom one was taken about 1975, by which time I was just angry, and the mask was well and truly up.

I rarely smiled on any of the photo's I have of me whilst in the Royal Navy.

Physical training was another opportunity for men to be humiliated. Our kit was the first noticeable way in which you would feel somewhat foolish. Long blue (button fly) shorts (with turn ups of course, which were handy for putting cigarette butts in), an old-fashioned button Collar long sleeve sports top, long blue stockings, and plimsolls. Between the bottom of my shorts, and the top of my stockings was literally no more than one inch of flesh. Most of my kit was far to big for me, at five foot two inches and seven stone in weight, I had only just been accepted under the understanding that I would grow some more.

Then came the interviews with your divisional officer. He would tell you how well you were doing, and that you were now a highly trained individual. The Navy had invested

Life in the balance

thousands of pounds in this training, and when the day came that you left, you would be in high demand. I would leave those interviews convinced that it would be at the least totally selfish of me to even consider leaving after all the Navy had done for me.

Yet still, deep down inside, I wanted to go home. I wanted to say how I really felt, but I couldn't. I was convinced that any love I received was conditional, I had to be seen to achieve by all. A year or so later my grandmother died. I was now serving on my first ship, still only just seventeen. Gran had lived with us all my life, and she looked after us while mum and dad were at work. I asked my Divisional officer for compassionate leave to which he responded, "Don't be so stupid, it's only your grandmother for goodness sake. You can't go running home to mummy and daddy at every little mishap." Again, instead of either explaining my situation or even disagreeing with him, I buckled under and in a sense ran away from confrontation. I could have insisted on leave as I was still under eighteen and therefore legally, at that time, under my Parents authority. I was also learning to keep my true feelings to myself, for every time I allowed them to surface, it seemed to me that they attracted nothing but either derision, or prompted someone to attack me in some way.

Even then, inside myself were developing seeds of self-hatred. I hated my weakness, I hated myself for allowing the abuses of various kinds, I hated being at the mercy of others, I hated being a victim, I hated having no control in my life – I hated! So young, and yet already full of 'unresolved conflicts,' which would continue to grow in compliment and in depth. Little did I know, even after becoming a Christian, the damage that these unresolved conflicts could do. How even already 'thought patterns' were developing that would eventually become firmly established as strongholds, which would need to be challenged and brought down.

Life in the balance

I have discovered that I had many counterparts in the bible. People, who for various reasons, came to a point in their life when they felt the only answer was to run. Moses, running through a wilderness, to a quiet life in Midian, trying to live with his failure as a self-appointed deliverer.

Elijah. Leaving his servant, on the run, the man of power for the hour, who entered a 'burn out' experience. Jonah. Disobedient, angry, and sullen. Jacob. Running from a name, and into an encounter with God that would launch him into his new identity.

Yes, running away is a 'way' I suppose, but it's not God's way. God's way may well involve a wilderness, but in that wilderness is a road – a way that will lead us right into His presence.

In Moses' wilderness was an unusual bush, it came on a day when I am sure Moses perhaps felt that this would just be another unexciting, uneventful day.

Elijah's wilderness time lead him to a dark cave, and a meeting that was to bring him to a renewed experience with his Lord. Jonah of course ended up in the belly of a fish, giving him time to consider his way.

It's Jacob who I felt more akin to. Of course, I would never have wanted to admit to this until recently. I much preferred to liken myself to many of the heroes of the bible in my younger days, however, I have discovered that all of the heroes of faith had to discover Gods way for them, and learn to follow it.

We find in Genesis 32:22-31 Jacob experiencing something that would bring what in fact was a long journey to a kind of climax, a time when he would at last face the truth. It is so often the Truth encounter that we all dread, give us the power

Life in the balance

any day, that's probably what goes through our minds, if we are honest, when we ask God to change us. Just do it quick Lord! As we stand in the prayer line, not always realising that with many changes there is a process of learning, re-learning, breaking, rebelling, manipulating until finally, and sometimes suddenly, everything is brought to a head and we face the truth.

Many of us are not fully realising what is happening when we respond to a word, or we go forward in a meeting believing that we will somehow merely catch something coming from God through the minister, or perhaps we will instantly receive a revelation.

We need to understand that sometimes the master gardener is planting a seed. That seed needs to initially be received. It will then require gestation time, before it finally begins to sprout and appear, in what is to begin with perhaps, an immature state. It is this time, whilst the seed is still as it were in the earth, hidden, unseen, that we often have a problem. We wrongly assume that nothing is in fact happening; this can lead to real damage being done with regards to our faith.

Really I want to share with you the kind of experiences we have with God that often leave us with various different things. Jacob got a new name, a new destiny but he also got a limp, and a reminder of what it was all about. He had entered a time in his life when we have pictured for us a wrestling bout, some would say a 'laying hold of God,' oft' times in my case a desperate holding on, clinging to. There have been times I experienced what seemed to be conflict after conflict, trouble after trouble, and pain after pain until I was screaming out to God, "I will not let you go until you bless me."

Consequently, during these times, like many before us, I have often questioned Gods position in it all. Somehow deep down

Life in the balance

there has also been a conviction that there has to be a blessing in all of this. The truth is friends there is, but just like Israel discovered, Marah came before Elim, and God required them to drink from Marah for a purpose – in short, the purpose was to get Egypt out of Israel. He required them to drink from those waters in order that they might be purged, and then would come the cooler sweeter waters of Elim.

So many times, we want to by pass Marah and head directly to the sweet experiences not realising that in fact we are robbing ourselves of the incredible revelation of God. We look for short cuts, and most Pastors know the frustration of members who believe that a response for prayer will just do it! They often reject any notion of a process being initiated leading eventually to change.

The very thing that we run away from is often the very thing that we need in order for us to truly change. There are things about ourselves that we need to face up to. Not in order to come under any kind of condemnation or indeed to wallow in self pity. Nor is this that we might share our experiences to merely illicit human sympathy, in some kind of incestuous inward-looking pity party. No! Rather, that we might be able to learn, to perhaps even more fully appreciate the ways of the Lord, to recognise His incredible patience, His wonderful grace and mercy extended towards us as we go through the processes that at times can be so ugly. I have often looked back and been able to proclaim, "Father, how much you love me."

As a child, it took discipline from my father to stop me running away every time I encountered some kind of problem. I would like to be able to say that I learnt my lesson well, the trouble with discipline is, either we accept it and learn from it, or we inwardly chafe' and eventually make the same, or similar mistakes again. After my first successful experience at

Life in the balance

running away, further attempts, as I said, were dealt with in the first instance, by firm discipline, but eventually they were simply ignored.

I can recall on one or two occasions, after a 'dramatic exit' from the home, dad would simply say to mum, "he'll be back when he's hungry," and sure enough, I was. I would wander up and down the field at the rear of our home, knowing that dad could see me as he sat in the back garden reading his newspaper. I felt sure he would come and get me as he had before, but he never did. We all know that there are two ways of learning in our walk. Trustingly, as a child, holding on to His hand. Or with the 'bit and bridle,' stubbornly, at times needing to be dragged along.

Winston Churchill said, quote "When you feel you cannot continue in your position for another minute, and all that is in human power has been done, that is the moment when the enemy is most exhausted, and when one step forward will give you the fruits of the struggle you have borne." unquote

I have, and still am learning, that often the points I give in at and run from, have proven to be the opportunities that God gave for me to grow through. What we can so often perceive as being an intolerable moment in our lives, can often be the point or place God has needed for us to arrive at in order for Him to bring us to a moment of growth.

You know, in truth, it is a human trait that almost expects life to be 'nice, quiet, peaceful, contented and the like.' The sheer pressure of it being anything other than that can be the motivation that causes us to go on the run. The problem with that is what is it going to take to get you to stop running?

Life in the balance

Members of my first training class in the 'Benbow' division, at HMS Raleigh Torpoint.

I am in the front row Centre. The chap on My left used to be a Boxer, and decided To take me under his wing and teach me a few tricks. I do not think I listened all that well, judging by the fact I have had my nose broken more than once.

Life in the balance

Chapter Two - Pressure

I believe it is entirely possible to be on the run without even knowing it. Even when we exhibit personality traits that; to others are obvious in their ugliness. Insecurities, that crop up time and time again, all which point to the need for that person perhaps to do some facing up, we can be to an extent, blinded to these things.

Intimate fellowship with God is the first and most important means through which we discover these areas. The next means is through intimate fellowship with fellow members of the body of Christ. The alternative is often through following a course that is simply out of the will of God for our lives.

There are times in our lives when we become; comfortable, rebellious, simply disobedient, and even ignorant of the need for change. In these instances, we so often cling to our lives and want to live them on our terms, not realising that in doing so we fail to appropriate life on Gods terms. In my own life I would say that God, on the whole has been very gentle, keeping His finger on sensitive areas. I knew the day would come that I would have to face up to certain issues, but I would avoid it as much as possible, until Father would have to increase the weight of His finger, in order to force the issue somewhat.

This truth is more often than not revealed to us during times of pressure. Of course, we all live to varying degrees under pressure. Pressure can have all kinds of effects upon us, some good, some not so good. However, there is one thing that pressure is sure to do eventually and that is to magnify, and what it magnifies is what is really there.

Life in the balance

Pressure in fact is normal to every day living as well as the Christian life. When I tune my guitar, the correct amount of tension is required to bring the correct note, too much tension of course can cause the string to snap, and not enough will cause it to emit the wrong note. A diamond has the form that it has because of the pressure it has endured. The more pressure matter can withstand, it would seem, the more valuable it becomes. The same can be true of people.

When we are under pressure or living under perhaps an inordinate amount of stress, the kind that has actually ceased to motivate us in a positive way, but rather is gradually eroding our ability to cope any longer, we are in danger of burning out. You will recall that even the great prophet Elijah went through a time like this after his momentous confrontation with the prophets of Baal.

He suffered in many of the ways we also suffer on the road to 'burn out.' He went through severe depression, despair, a sense of resignation, failure and inferiority. These things are revealed in his own words, "I have had enough, LORD," he said. "Take my life; I am no better than my ancestors." 1 Kings 19:4

He crashed eventually under a 'juniper tree' where he experiences an angelic foot that kicks him back into life in order to 'get fed, get up, and go forth' on a journey of discovery. Ahead of him lays a cave where he experiences a time of judgement – not with respect to his eternal judgement, but rather a time of "krisis" from where we get our word crisis.

I wonder what would have happened if Elijah had argued with the angel and simply refused to get up and get fed? I have noticed since becoming a Christian that there are those who would simply settle for some human sympathy, rather than respond with Holy Spirit courage to the promptings of God.

Life in the balance

If Elijah, in his depression, had refused to get up and get fed at that point, he would never have gone forth and consequently would have failed to re-discover his intimacy with God. God did his part. Elijah needed to respond. He could have been offended of course at the way the angel got his attention.

People get offended when they hear a sermon, they know it has application to their own situation, but they would have rather the answer come enshrouded in human sympathy and spiritual clucking, if you take my meaning. There can be severe consequences if we refuse the promptings of God. Or if we shut out Gods voice.

It is at Horeb of course where Elijah once again experiences intimacy with God through the still small voice. God's question to Elijah is, "what are you doing here?" Elijah keeps giving answers at that point to 'why' but that is not what God asked him.

Friend, God knows 'why' we get to where we get, what He wants to know from us is whether we know 'what' we are doing there. Are we really seeing and understanding what the purpose of God is yet? We go on the run (have we discovered why?) we are under pressure (from what?).

You see, there are moments in our walk with God where, for whatever reason, He allows times of crisis/pressure in order to show us (magnify) what is actually going on within us, as well as the more obvious things that are taking place regarding our circumstances.

I remember Sheila and I going through a learning curve in the area of trusting God to provide. I was in for some embarrassing lessons. I had an attitude that had developed that basically believed that God will only provide your needs, and

Life in the balance

by that I meant the things we need to literally live. However, I seriously doubted He would go much beyond that. This attitude had developed due to being exposed to some extreme prosperity teaching that had led me to see God as a provider, no matter what.

One day, after reading a particular book where I learnt that if there was something wrong with your car you could pray for it and it would be healed. I went outside to my rusty old Ford Escort Mk 1 and prayed over a huge hole in the sill. Two weeks later I noted that a huge clump of moss had grown where the hole was. Sheila laughed and said, "You weren't specific enough, you didn't ask for metal." So, I swung too far the other way and decided that God did not bother Himself with little things like this. I read lots of books about missionaries who lived lives of piety and went without, suffering in some cases terribly. That is how I would be. I equated this as spirituality, to be spiritual meant being poor and going without. So, the attitude that was magnified in my life was obvious and was going to be dealt with.

Corrie Ten Boom once commented, concerning some missionaries who were suffering terribly in the area of provision, "They have given all, but have not claimed all."

Sheila had been purchasing some microwave cookbooks; they were weekly magazines that cost quite a lot of money, in the days when we were on a very low wage. I was very good at budgeting our finances, and so, as we did not have a microwave of our own I considered this as a waste of money. I asked Sheila why she was buying them, and she responded by telling me that one day we may have a microwave, and that they would then be useful to us.

I recall rounding on her and saying, "we could never afford a microwave." You see deep down I was angry with God, I

Life in the balance

resented being on such a tight budget, I thought we deserved better. Well, the telephone rang almost as soon as the words left my mouth. I answered, and a friend asked me if we had a microwave. I had that feeling, you know, the one where you know that God has just been listening to your conversation and is about to get out of the box you tried to put Him in. They had a microwave that was virtually brand new and they gave it to us as a gift, in fact we have only just changed it after some thirteen years. It is still going strong and is housed in one of the Churches kitchens.

One would have thought that was enough to convince me, but I had to learn the same lesson again, this time with a video machine. I was convinced that video machines were an unnecessary expense, and besides which, "we could never afford one." Sheila and I had a similar conversation to the one we had concerning the microwave, and that very same evening I was approached and given a video machine.

Later that year God took the lesson several steps forward, He provided for us in such an amazing way that we were left literally embarrassed by His lavish nature. It was getting close to Christmas and we had nothing. No money, nothing in our cupboards, the challenge for us was what would we now believe about God? What would our attitude be should we not be able to provide anything special for our children that year? I dreaded trying to explain to two small children that because we were serving the Lord, there would be no treats this year. I struggled with the two extremes, trusting God for your needs, not your greed's.

After reading about George Muller in the book, "Delighted in God," we both decided this was something we would keep between God and ourselves. We didn't plead, beg or demand, we simply waited on Him. We would simply be content with whatever He decided. One morning my sister contacted me to

Life in the balance

inform me that she had got us a Christmas cake, due to the fact that the factory she worked at had a number left over they were giving to the staff.

We were dancing around the bedroom, we had a cake, we had nothing else, but we did have a cake. We received a letter from the council informing us they had made a mistake with our rent calculations, and we owed them £200. God already had the matter in hand when a cheque arrived which paid it off. We also received a 13llb turkey from a couple in the church; I jokingly nudged Sheila and said that all we needed now was a leg of Pork. Sure enough, the next morning another couple turned up with a leg of pork.

We had told no one about our situation, only God knew of our situation. Well for the next few days we had at least four hampers arrive, financial gifts amounting to hundreds of pounds, food vouchers, gifts of all kinds, it just went on and on. Each time someone gave us something they said the same thing, "God told us to give you this." Eventually we had to start packing the car and go and deliver stuff to others in the Church, and it kept coming until we prayed, "It is enough Lord." Suddenly it stopped. The following year we began to receive the recommended salary, therefore we did not need God to provide in the same way, and you know something, He didn't.

And my lesson was learnt. Some might say, "I wouldn't mind learning that lesson myself." Well maybe so, however it goes both ways. Once you realise how generous God really is, you are obligated to seek to be that way yourself aren't you?

My attitude was magnified during those lessons, I recognised it (eventually) and sought to seek God in changing me, and I am pleased to say He has. Contentment in all kinds of areas can often be a difficult lesson to learn.

Life in the balance

In 2 Thessalonians chapter 1 v4 we have the apostle commending the church over their perseverance and faith amidst times of persecution and trials. In other words, here are the attitudes he sees 'magnified' during times of intense pressure and crisis.

When we ourselves experience times of crisis or intense pressure it is an opportunity to see magnified both good and not so good responses in us. Either way there is an opportunity for growth.

Jesus often allowed His disciples to experience times of pressure in order to reveal to them areas where they needed to grow. God's discipline is never to humiliate us but rather to reveal to us clearly areas He is concerned about. Let's face it, if we are honest oft' times we are simply not listening to Him as we should.

When we embark upon a road of 'running away' it is often because we encounter something we do not want to face up to. So, off we go, on a detour, a way of getting around, sometimes getting out, often even going back. The very thought of going through is just too much for us.

So often we base our fears upon a presupposition that is simply untrue, due to the fact that we are not seeing clearly. I presumed that should I leave the Navy, both my parents would perceive that as failure, and the attention I felt I had would be lost. Now although my parents were proud of me, their pride in me was not conditional on me remaining away from home. So, I chose a path based on the assumption that my parent's love was conditional, and that the condition was that I succeeded in the career I had now chosen.

Life in the balance

That is the place where our heavenly father will almost certainly return us. The place where we sought our way, in preference to His. I have discovered personally that God has allowed me to go so far down a road of distraction, or even disobedience for so long. However, I find that the pressure of being 'out of His will' is far greater than any perceived troubles, mountains, or obstacles that arise from walking 'in His will.'

Elijah's moment of truth if you like at Horeb came when God kept asking the question, "What are you doing here?" God knew all about the process that had brought Elijah there. He didn't need reminding of all the things from his point of view he had endured, or his limited opinions on the situation in the nation. God was seeking something far more important. "What are you doing here Elijah?" Here, meaning, this cave, this moment, right now! I have found that, like Elijah, when I arrive at, lets call it crash point, that is the question that needs to be asked and answered. What am I doing here now?

Elijah's problem was not what he thought it was, it wasn't that his zeal was lacking, or Israel's faithlessness, or the killing of the prophets, or his sense of isolation and so on. It was when Elijah heard the gentle whisper that he pulled his cloak over his face. Elijah needed the presence of the Lord, somehow, during all his great battles, all his zeal, all his doing, the intimate presence of God was in some way lacking in him. He had forgotten that the very greatest blessing anyone can receive, is an encounter with the Lord.

Church leader, your zeal for God may be commendable, maybe you have got a church where you think you are the only one really pulling the weight, to a degree maybe you even think they are out to get you! You can probably even come up with the goods on a Sunday, bring a great word. But are you hearing the word of the Lord for you? Are you enjoying that

Life in the balance

intimacy that we all long for? Are we facing up to the right question? Or simply listing all the reasons over and over as to why we think it has all gone wrong?

Now pressure can come from 'without' and from 'within.' "For when we came into Macedonia, this body of ours had no rest, but we were harassed at every turn--conflicts on the outside, fears within." 2 Corinthians 7:5

I have often made the mistake of judging my future according to my past. We must not allow past failures to hold us back, dwelling upon failure only robs us of our future potential, and even the joys of our present. We also need to realise afresh at times that Gods power is perfected in weakness, not strength.

Oh, broken reed sometimes your life seems battered down,
Tossed on a sea of circumstance and shadows gown.
So, bruised and bent, you wonder if you'll stand again,
And whether life and all your dreams will simply wain.

Oh, broken reed can you not see your Fathers hand,
He speaks the word, He binds the wound it's time to stand,
It seems to you your times are oft' like shifting sands.
But feel His touch and you will know He understands.

Oh, dying flame, your lights so dim you're in the shade,
The smoke of fear it stings your eyes, your tears cascade,
And when you lose you wonder if He'll stay around,
But thoughts like that just do not help they'll bring you down.

Oh, dying flame can you not feel his gentle breath?
His precious wind fans into flame, removes the death,
I know it's hard to understand how He can care,
Just believe in Fathers love He's always there.

Life in the balance

He won't cut off oh broken reed so do not fear,
He won't snuff out oh dying flame you're much to dear,
His steadfast love is the one thing that never flies,
He holds the reed, He feeds the flame, they will not die!

Song by D Crabb

Life in the balance

Chapter Three – Pressing on through Pressure

I love the attitude of Sir Winston Churchill. A man who knew incredible moments of failure in his life, yet somehow, he maintained a positive outlook when he said, "We are all worms. But I do believe that I am a glow-worm." Indeed, when his moment in history came he was found to be ready for the task.

It is also believed that Winston had a model that was kept on his desk, a beautiful model of a ship, made entirely from burnt matchsticks. The illustration being clear, in that God is able to construct beautiful lives from what is ostensibly, the burnt out remains of lives that in their own strength have literally almost blown themselves out.

There is no doubt that once we embark upon the road of faith that we begin to face resistance and opposition from without and from within. No wonder we are called into fellowship, it would be impossible for any of us to stand alone.

Paul the apostle knew what it was to face resistance from the enemy, yet he also knew what it was to experience conflicts within. When I say within I mean both within the body of Christ, and also the conflicts of doubt, and fears within ourselves. I once remember a preacher saying, "Goliath never bothered to spend too much time trying to verbally discourage David, he didn't need to, his 'brothers' had already done that."

The most painful and difficult conflicts to deal with are those that occur within the body of Christ. Satan takes a perverse pleasure in using Gods children to do his dirty work. He will seek all kinds of ways to inflict as much damage as possible to a faithful one before making any kind of direct assault upon

Life in the balance

them. This softening up process often occurs through believers who are not being as alert in the spiritual realm as they should be.

There seems to be an attitude in the body of Christ that manifests whenever someone dares to start climbing as it were. They will do one of three things; cheer them on to greater things, join them in the climb, or shoot them from below to bring them back down to their level. Some are like Jonathan and his armour bearer, climbing the hill to attack the Philistines. Some are like King Saul, sitting under the Pomegranate tree forever making plans, talking but never doing.

Paul experienced all three attitudes, but he did not make the mistake of allowing himself to become cynical in spirit. Neither must we. None of us are perfect, we are all in a constant state of learning (or we should be) that is what disciples are, learners, followers. We must be constantly aware that our battle is not with flesh and blood, but with principalities and powers.

Jesus, when encountering even well-meaning opposition to the purpose of God dealt with the spirit behind the words, He did not aim any salvos as it were at people. There have been times that I have preached very challenging messages that have stirred up responses that have not been entirely positive. Sadly, the recipients of frustration, even anger have often been my wife or even my children. This can be one of the most difficult things for a Pastor and his family to deal with. Offence carries with it a 'bitter sting' that can lead to the defilement of many.

Pastor Jim McConnell from the Whitewell Church in Northern Ireland once preached a stirring message entitled, "The Stink or the Storm." The point he made very clearly was it is better to be in the stink of the Ark, than the storm outside. The

Life in the balance

analogy is very clear. Some of us seem to live in a fantasy world where everything is wonderful all of the time. God's people always treat us as we want to be treated, our circumstances are always positive, and the enemy leaves us alone. If that is your experience I think you need to read the words of scripture again, "In fact, everyone who wants to live a godly life in Christ Jesus will be persecuted," 2 Tim 3:12

"We must go through many hardships to enter the kingdom of God," Acts 14:22.

Sadly, many Christians will settle for something less than what God has in mind for them. As soon as they encounter hardship of some kind they begin to allow themselves to be conformed to their surroundings rather than seek to change them through Godly confrontation.

We can be in danger of trying to find the path of least resistance. Jesus taught us that following in His footsteps would mean things like, carrying our own cross, denying self, resisting the devil, being obedient, suffering for His sake, putting our old self life to death and the like.

In the West we like to build into our lives ease and security, carefully designing our lives in such a way as to avoid any hardship, not that I am advocating voluntary hardship, or some kind of pseudo, so called spiritual masochism. But we are in danger if we begin to trust our plans and programs more than we do the Lord.

It is entirely possible that the right path, the godly path is the path of most resistance! So many have lost their way, because they assumed that the correct path was the one that offered little, or no resistance at all.

Life in the balance

Recently my wife and I went through a time in our lives of prolonged resistance, attack, opposition, and criticism, almost everything you could think of happened in a very short space of time.

We had only just come out of a time of real testing; we had just moved out of the Church house and purchased our own home. Sheila's father had a prolonged illness, which had involved her visiting him everyday in hospital for many months. I had just recovered from what was a cancer scare resulting in a 'subcutaneous mastectomy' (partial removal of breast). On the same day both my wife's father and I had operations. Poor Sheila was in Rugby one minute visiting her dad, and in Nuneaton the next visiting me.

When I came out of hospital, Sheila literally crashed. She was exhausted in every way, physically and emotionally. Sheila's dad eventually died, and at the same time we had also experienced some fairly serious leadership problems resulting in various people leaving the church. I did not recover too well from the operation, the consultant had told me to take a minimum of three weeks off, however, I was well into martyr mode, and so after the weekend I was back into work. This resulted in me having to have my wound drained on three or four different occasions, which was a very distressing procedure.

Apart from the normal pressures of pastoral life, we were also suffering financially after a number of unexpected costs hit us all at once. We didn't share this with anyone, because so often a Pastor's motives can be suspected when he shares his family's needs.

Sheila and I began to experience a loss of confidence in all kinds of ways. You begin to ask a lot of questions, Gods faithfulness, relationships you thought were rock solid are

Life in the balance

shaken, the absolute confidence we thought we had regarding our calling was also severely shaken. By that time, we were both, to an extent, looking for potential ways out. We were angry, hurting, and confused, yet also still hoping that God would change things. We wanted God to simply make things better for us, to give us a protracted time of peace and blessing. The irony is that even with all these things taking place, when asked how I was I would just say, fine! I would discover positive things to relate, I would speak positive things for that is what I thought was expected from me spiritually. It was also what I had learnt over many years, to bury my true feelings.

The following year began with the news that both my parents had been diagnosed with terminal cancers. I also developed a virus that kept me off work for a period of five weeks.

Moving into the year we had our daughter's wedding in the April which brought a number of stressful problems we had not banked on, including some personal attacks on members of our family that proved to be very difficult to deal with. Our finances were also hit again at that time with some more unexpected costs.

We sank even lower, yet at the same time sought to maintain a brave face and a 'business as usual' attitude. We were almost staggering towards our holiday, almost seeing it as the change that we needed, fooled into believing that afterwards everything would be better. There was additional conflict in both of our hearts, as we were talking between ourselves very much about a possible new ministry, not realising that in truth we wanted a 'way out.'

We took a holiday in the June and on returning found our car had been broken into and seriously vandalised, it was subsequently written off. We lost quite a lot of money on that.

Life in the balance

A week later our home was hit by lightning causing utter devastation, and requiring us to move into a hotel for two weeks and then into rented accommodation for about six months. It was a total mess. The gable end wall was damaged, many of the ceilings had fallen in, our son's bedroom was totally wrecked, as a fire had started, most of the electrical appliances were destroyed, the roof was damaged. We were just numb, yet also trying to be a good witness. The press in particular enjoyed reporting this, trying to bring an angle to the story. Their question was, "Is this an act of God?" Our question to them was, "We will answer that, but first of all, do you believe in God?"

So, it turned to our advantage in that we were able to witness to Gods faithfulness. The sad part of it all was the reaction of some Christians. Some just wanted to be able to take the position that we had obviously done something terribly wrong to receive this. We were told that it must be the 'judgement of God' for living in a 'panelled house,' actually it was a simple end of terrace. There were encouragements too, the first thing the Fire Chief said to Sheila when we returned home to find our home in pieces, was, "you must be Christians, normally when this sort of thing happens, people go to pieces."

There were also some amusing moments in all of this. Just a few hours after the fire brigade had left, we had to ensure the power supply was disconnected, the water was turned off, and generally needed to pack a few bags with some clothes and belongings, we then heard a strange buzzing noise.

We could not locate it anywhere. We were listening to radiators, had our ears pressed up against walls, wondering what on earth this new problem could be. In frustration we decided just to leave it, after all, what else could go wrong apart from the house falling down? It was already in a terrible state, ceilings had dropped in, the gable end wall was coming

Life in the balance

away, and the roof was in an awful state, all the electrics and appliances were destroyed, what could one more buzz do?

Just as I picked up a holdall to leave the buzzing grew louder. It seemed to be coming from the holdall? I opened it up to discover that my electric toothbrush was switched on, making this buzzing noise. We both just collapsed with laughter.

Sheila had been marvellous, and although her home lay in utter ruin, she maintained a positive disposition, believing still that in someway there was purpose in it all. However, just like me she was, to an extent, putting on a brave face. I would worry how much of that she was doing for my sake. Although we were both still 'praising the Lord' deep within there were questions developing concerning God's faithfulness. I had awareness that there was something much deeper going on that I simply could not see.

Of course, we both still had parents to look after as well. Sheila was visiting her mum almost daily, and had been since her dad died. I was daily visiting mum and dad as they both went through their respective treatments. Radiotherapy and Chemotherapy, and although they were both so brave, it was horrible seeing them suffer as they did. Eventually they both decided enough was enough, they were ready to meet with the Lord and decided they would have no further treatment.

Around this time, perhaps a little before, I was offered an opportunity to possibly move Church. This was unusual, for in all my time in ministry I had never before been offered anything. Strangely enough our previous Pastor, David Khan, had been ministering at the church that weekend. One of the things he asked was this, "are you just going for success, or are you going for Gods glory?" I knew in my heart that it was the glory of God that we both desperately wanted, and we

Life in the balance

decided to be patient and hang in there, for neither of us had a peace about leaving Rugby.

Our son was moved into my sister in laws home, and we moved into a hotel for two weeks and then a rented house for six months. Almost immediately another problem in the church began to develop which could have caused major difficulties, and resulted again in more people leaving the church.

Both of our children had stopped attending church, disillusioned by the attacks they had experienced from Christian's. My son had turned to drugs, it began to seem as though our whole world had been turned upside down. We thank God that only now that he is through this and going on with God, have we been made more aware just how serious his situation had become. We were reeling. I had also been struggling with inner conflicts and so I was coming closer and closer to a burn out experience. I would lay awake at night worrying about our children they weren't bad kids, and they were sincere in their attempts at living the Christian life. It seemed so unfair that they had received so many knocks in life. Where was God in all of this? The more I asked questions like that, the further away He seemed to be. The more I sought to gain control, the more it seemed our lives went out of control.

My daughter had a very bad experience at work, involving someone threatening to rape her, she had been experiencing a problem for some time through sexual harassment, and now it was getting very nasty. The company she worked for did nothing to help or protect her in anyway. She came under terrible attack. For some reason the whole work force turned against her, leaving messages like, "sack the vicar's daughter," daubed all over the toilet walls.

Life in the balance

The person who had perpetrated the sexual harassment was seen as the victim, after all, it was just 'a bit of fun.' Constantly telling her what he would like to do to her, showing her pornographic images. Sharing with his friend's things he had downloaded from the internet. Although she made all the correct approaches to the company to have this matter resolved, she was hindered at every point. Her doctor who was very concerned for her, as we were ourselves, signed her off work for over six months, due to her suffering with a terrible bout of depression. Normally our daughter was so bubbly, gifted and full of life, now it seemed as though all the life had been knocked out of her. Her confidence was affected, she would once be ministering regularly, now she was rarely even at church. On the odd occasions she came to church again, an insensitive comment would knock her back.

It seemed as though one moment we were positive, the next confused, at times we were simply going on. The holiday had been the best we had ever experienced; yet the benefits it seemed were lost as soon as we returned. The whole thing seemed so cruel. I failed to recognise at the time how demanding I was becoming in my prayer life. All I could pray about were the problems; it was almost all I could see. I must confess I was also angry with Christians. Sheila and I had spent so much of our lives 'being there' for others, now it seemed to us as though few were really interested in what was happening in our lives.

Finally, at the end of the November I broke. I was left convinced that I was finished, my ministry was over and people would never be able to respect my leadership again. I was leaning hard on Sheila, and I began to realise what this must have been doing to her, as she watched the one she loves slowly but surely going under.

Life in the balance

At break down point I had to go to the church with the elders to write a letter to a couple I had offended. It almost seemed as though I was going to the office to collect my things and leave. I remember looking at the church building and thinking, "I wonder if I will ever go in there again?" It was a frightening thought. I collected a number of things for by that time my Regional Superintendent had already told me I would be having a break. It was a relief actually to know that now we were literally in free fall as it were. I sensed a bitterness arising in my heart that I was desperately trying to suppress, yet if truth be said not really succeeding.

I will never forget the look on Sheila's face as I left the home with the elders. My heart was almost bursting in distress as I thought back to the time I got the sack in my job as a manager. I couldn't help but compare the two experiences. I began to wonder if that was the simple truth, I was just a failure. Still, I simply pretended I was fine, I could not bring myself to bear my heart, my pain to those around me. I now try to imagine what it must have been like for these men who had served with me for so many years. These were and are men who love me and respected me. One of them had been to visit immediately on hearing the news and sat with us and wept and prayed over us.

People around us were on the whole sympathetic and supportive, yet, it felt as though we could sense they were confused, disappointed in me perhaps, and so I withdrew. I stayed away from the church completely for about five weeks, and avoided fellowship, even with those I was previously close to. My feelings, it seemed to me, were confirmed when I returned to work, when a member made it quite clear that in their opinion I had just enjoyed a nice five or six week break. That attitude hurt me deeply, and I worried that others perhaps saw things in the same way. After all, this person in particular

Life in the balance

was someone I had stood with during their own moments of perceived failure.

A few weeks later my mother died, it was an awful weekend, although we knew this time had been approaching you are never really prepared when that time arrives. Mum had grown increasingly weaker, and despite dad's valiant efforts in caring for her, one weekend she had to be admitted to hospital. She had begun fitting, and eventually it was discovered a secondary cancer had grown in her brain. After a struggle, mum passed into the Lords presence.

Recognising I was in no real state to take the funeral, I had already arranged for a colleague who knew mum to do the service. In fact, he was held up on the motorway, which meant me taking the greater part of the service. He arrived in time to do the address, just as the tributes had finished. In fact, that situation helped to restore some of the confidence I was now lacking. Because I was forced to face this, I discovered strength I didn't realise I had.

I also realised that in truth my calling was still there, and that indeed I wanted to continue serving the Lord. A few days later we had to move back to our now restored home. And so we entered another year hoping and praying that things would get better. At this time God also began showing me my heart. That is, I began to see how all I was ever asking God for was relief, a better life, and nicer circumstances. God had something far greater in mind.

I knew that I needed help to discover why this was going on in my life, and so I contacted a friend, who is pastor of an evangelical church. Although I appreciated his skills, it was his friendship, and confidence in me that began a healing process, and in that, enlightenment began to take place. He moved alongside me as a Barnabas, and made it clear that as

Life in the balance

far as he was concerned, he was a 'friend' with me in all that I would go through.

I could see the need to understand myself better. The 'life events' that we had endured in such a short space of time was incredible. The Holmes Rahe scale revealed we were off the scale, and had been for a long time. Counsellors often use the Holmes Rahe scale as a means of predicting the possibility of illness caused by too much stress. A points system is worked out, giving so many points to various kinds of life events.

Less than 150 points and there is a 30% chance of stress related illness, 150-299 points and there is a 50% chance of stress related illness, over 300 points and there is an 80% chance. A 'conservative' estimate brought our points total towards the end of the year to 363.

We should have reached out for help, but we didn't think there was anyone to reach out to, so we consequently sought to deal with things ourselves. There was a major lesson here for me, for there were plenty of people who were willing to help, I just failed to seek them out. David Carr from Solihull was very timely in his love and support, as was our General Superintendent John Glass, and other members of the Elim National Leadership Team who took the time to ring us up and check on us. Gordon Neale also took time to keep a check on us, ringing up, keeping contact with the elders. George Canty had also made contact after the lightning strike on our home, a timely letter sharing many personal insights from his own life was very helpful.

I spent the next couple of months trying to repair fences in relationships that had been damaged through my burn out, and eventually went on holiday exhausted. Sadly, again another attack on my family ensued, and on returning from our holiday a few weeks later my father died, suddenly.

Life in the balance

In all of this there were good things happening, but it was getting difficult to concentrate on them, and even at times recognise that God was still working for us. My son had a renewed experience with the Lord, resulting in him coming off the drugs and smoking, and finding himself a lovely wife. People in the Elim movement had also responded with kindness and generosity, we saw a lot of 'practical help.'

Suffering the bible tells us produces. As we saw in the previous chapter, what it produces will eventually be manifested in some way. My personal conviction is that if you are still pressing on you are doing the will of God. Either we will press on, or be squeezed into the world's mould by being pressed 'out.'

I was still maintaining an attitude that was almost demanding, that God wanted me to have a 'nice pleasant life' that did not include problems and difficulties.

The road we walk is a narrow one, making it difficult to travel at times. Some of these situations we encountered could have been avoided. Certainly, the things that were magnified in my own life could have been covered over, ignored. I could have re-erected the defence mechanisms, opted out, sought a new ministry; there were numerous routes I could have taken.

I hope I am not misunderstood here, but I could also have decided to remain depressed. Even amid all the confusion that one experiences during depression, I knew without a doubt there were many issues to be resolved, and until they were resolved I would continue to experience this reactive condition. It was indeed like being in a dark pit that had a ladder in it, to climb the ladder would require a lot of effort, but each step would bring me closer to the light, and the way out. I remembered that our Lord called us, His is a high calling

Life in the balance

and there are some things that actually have to be pressed in to if we are to continue onwards.

Pressing into is a proactive thing. Sadly today because of our culture of convenience, if something is costly fewer people pursue it, especially if it means hard work. That is why there are so many 'cranky Christians' in the church today. They have chosen an easier road that does not require them to face up to issues in their lives, they settle into their personalities not realising the personalities are often the product of a diseased root. Every fruit tree has its own root.

There are folks who are constantly 'hurt or offended' Anger, malice, greed, lack of self control, lusts of all kinds (not just sexual), prickliness, controlling or manipulating behaviour, pride all these things have their roots, and only those pressing on will dare to face them.

This book is all about refusing to take the so-called easier route, the escape route can often be an appealing prospect with its promise of an easier life perhaps. However, it is paved with the characteristics of luke-warmness, compromise, apathy and self preservation.

Jesus taught us that mountains must be removed, not detoured around, not feared, and can I say without wanting to be misunderstood not necessarily even climbed over. If a mountain is going to be removed it must first of all be faced up to.

I have discovered that at moments like these you need to discover who the Barnabas' are in your life. They are the ones who stick with you no matter what flaws are exposed in you, as you face these things in your life.

Life in the balance

My best friend, apart from the Lord, has always been my wife. In fact, though now we have been married over 43 years, after we first became Christians in 1984, after seven years of marriage, I knew then that there were things I needed to be able to share with her, but I was scared.

I desperately wanted to tell her about the abuse, but my fear was that she would change in her attitude towards me. Eventually, I did tell her, and her response convinced me that she was not only my life partner, but also one whom I could trust implicitly. She wrapped her arms around me, looked up to me and said, "That is what a real man of God is, someone who is willing to face the biggest fears in his life." I knew then that she would never be disillusioned with me, real friends never are. They do not become disillusioned with you, because they had no illusions about you in the first place. They are fellow travellers, realising there have been and will continue to be times in their own lives when they too will need a friend.

In fact, a few years later, both Sheila and I shared at a much deeper level with one another, further things that had happened in our lives. The effect of this was to draw us even closer together as we experienced the joy of unconditional love, the reality of open-heart contact.

When being interviewed for the Elim ministry, Sheila was asked a question by one of the interviewers. "What do you most admire about your husband?" Her response was simply this, "His heart." That answer seemed to be more than satisfactory. I thank God for the joy of having a wife who knows me so well, yet is able to see beyond the things that could be so offensive to others who do not know you so well.

Paul had a realistic view of himself when he said, "Not that I have already obtained all this, or have already been made perfect, but I press on to take hold of that for which Christ

Life in the balance

Jesus took hold of me." Phil 3:12. The key word for us here is 'press' Paul speaking by the Holy Spirit is saying that he is working through all kinds of resistance. We do not just stumble into these things, we must press into them. He went on to say in verse 14, "I press on toward the goal to win the prize for which God has called me heavenward in Christ Jesus."

One more quote from Sir Winston Churchill who said regarding truth, "Man will occasionally stumble over the truth, but most of the time he will pick himself up and continue on."

Like you I have attended the seminars, I have listened to the tapes, watched the video's, enjoyed the conferences, gone forward for prayer, read the books. I have come away sometimes thinking that on the intellectual level I have understood the truth, and in pride at times acted as though I owned it. I am learning still that knowledge is good, but the great test comes when it is time to apply that knowledge.

One of my favourite texts is, "Do your best to present yourself to God as one approved," 2 Tim 2:15. To press on into truth will sometimes require you to face the truth about your self. I want to make it very clear however, I do not believe it to be healthy to examine ourselves with a view to try and simply analyse. The only point in discovering an unhealthy root is in order to pluck it out.

As someone once said, "Get cut get healed and get over it!" That remark was made within the context of Israel and the generation that needed to be circumcised.

Life in the balance

Chapter Four– Facing the Past

"Oh, son you know how long that it has been,
Since you spent some time to share with me your dreams,
I've never interfered, I've not complained,
I was hoping that you'd talk with me again.

I thought I'd made it clear right from the start,
The love I want must come straight from the heart,
Yet still you fight, you often turn away,
And all I've done is bless you more each day.

I love you with a love that's pure and whole,
You have felt it as it reached into your soul,
In that place where once I knew an open door,
Another, stands that you say you need much more.

Well I want to say I love you all the same,
I won't let you go you'll always bear my name,
'cause the love I give it cost me grief and pain,
And the life I give is promised to remain.

So lift your head my child and come to me,
I won't force my hand I've made you to be free,
Your life is made of choices, loss and gain,
But one thing that will always be the same,
Is my love"…………………

Song – D Crabb

There are things in life that happen to us! Just as there are things that we do, either to ourselves, or to others, that we too have to take responsibility for. The process of facing up is so

Life in the balance

difficult for it also involves taking responsibility. In addition to this is the need to learn how to forgive, either others or indeed ourselves.

When I first gave my life to Jesus I just knew deep down inside that there were immediately things that the Lord had his finger on. When I first became aware of this I was filled with a sense of foreboding, yet, almost at the same time there was an awareness that although the Lord intended to do something about these areas, it would be in His way and His time and that He would never take me beyond what I could bear.

As a runaway I never dreamt that I would run right into trouble! Most runaways believe that they are actually running away from trouble and running to a better life, that is rarely the case, if ever. You cannot run away from things that in fact are part of you!

I can remember on more than one occasion being in a meeting where the ministry time was concerning forgiveness, where perhaps one was encouraged to go back in time and forgive anyone who had hurt you or offended or even abused you in some way. I sincerely thought that was all there was to it. I can now see that it is not always as straightforward as that.

I had over the years developed so many masks, crusts, defence systems, ways of controlling or manipulating circumstances, all these things were designed to protect and needed to be dismantled. It was almost impossible to tell which was the real me, and which was that I had developed to protect myself.

I am beginning to appreciate just how wise our Father is, He knows just what to do and when – but believe me when I say that if we are determined to know Him more He will do whatever is necessary.

Life in the balance

The wonderful thing that I have discovered is that whilst our Father is able to see all that is wrong in us, He is also able to do so whilst seeing us in our 'completion.'

I have needed to come to understand that when God looks at me He is able to see me in my completed state as well as my incompletion. His viewpoint is the Eternal one mine is limited to lineal time and space. That is what makes Him God!

His desire is to have fellowship with us, for us to truly worship Him in spirit and in truth therefore anything false, even that built with what humanly may be considered a good motive, will be brought down. With God you do not need the masks, the protection, and certainly no one will ever control or manipulate Him.

So, good for you if you have managed to forgive someone, but remember, there may also be attitudes that you have developed because of abuse or hurt of some kind that also will need to be brought down. Strongholds are after all, thought patterns – once described by someone as a 'house of thoughts.' These attitudes have been developed over years and through much repetition and will need to be purged in the same way.

When I was first ever sexually abused as a six year old I became a victim, also a people pleaser and I learnt to an extent to live in fear. This was something that happened to me! A much older, distant relative led me to do things that at the time I had no understanding were wrong. Others in similar positions never go out looking for this kind of thing to happen to them, it would be offensive in the least to even suggest that. Thankfully this abuse did not go on over a protracted period of time, and to an extent it was largely forgotten about as I grew up. To forgive that person who first ever abused me was not 'for me' terribly difficult, because I did not realise how much damage had been done. I didn't think I was still carrying any

Life in the balance

kind of pain – it all seemed such a long time ago.

It wasn't until I began to acknowledge the personality traits and the ways in which I could so easily become a victim in conflict situations, a people pleaser as a Pastor, and fearful in heart when attacked that I realised how much damage had in fact been done. How I could so easily fall into an attitude where, in a sense, I would end up abusing myself. That is what we do when we do not believe the truth about ourselves.

It is a statistical fact that some who are abused can, if not helped, turn into abusers themselves. In my case, rather than seeking to abuse others, I abused myself further. I achieved this when as a young tender 15 year old, 5ft 2" tall, seven stone in weight, eyes of blue and a shock of blonde hair, I entered a world of adult men, this also became a traumatic experience for me, particularly with so many damaging personality traits already in place.

When I was next abused as a teenager, more serious damage was done, causing me to seek protection in the only way I could think of, that was to put on a mask, a front designed to keep others at bay, and to keep me in control.

Some of these masks of course were already in place. That was what had caused me to not only join the navy in the first place, and to continue, even though I hated being away from home. So, in order to remain I had to develop more masks and defence mechanisms.

For me the mask was to become in some ways obnoxious to others thereby keeping them at a distance, or at the least becoming to an extent an unknown, unpredictable quantity. This I achieved when drinking. Drink gave me a false kind of bravado, I became loud, even at times intimidating to others, often getting into fights or troubles of various kinds.

Life in the balance

I sought to prove myself in the arena of relationships and to gain a reputation as a womaniser, I further compounded this by entering a sordid world of pornography and sex shows, when in countries where that kind of thing thrived. I was, as far as anyone else was concerned, 'one of the boys.' When I came home on leave from the Navy, people would want to be around me, but I knew deep down inside it was only because they didn't really know me at all. They liked a personality that was nothing like the real me at all. I desperately wanted to be real, but I could not, I dare not. Of course, all of this only resulted in me hating myself even more, for inside I was a different person and therefore I had a major conflict going on all of the time.

To an extent I became what I thought and perceived others wanted me to become. Because I perceived my father as being rough and tough, I assumed that was what was required of me to fully receive his acceptance and his love. Many times, I had stood before my dad, and was chastised for being afraid, or not standing up for myself. I understand now, as an adult man, this was normal for my generation. So, I had to discover a way of being this, despite my sensitivity. It could have been disastrous.

Many times, I got myself into situations that could have had momentous consequences. On one occasion there was such a big fight in the mess deck of a ship I was currently serving on, involving knives and screwdrivers. I began to realise that I was entering a world that I would not be able to handle; I was walking a dangerous road that would require me to go all the way. This would ultimately involve me really hurting someone if I was not careful.

On several occasions I got myself into some potentially dangerous situations, as soon as I started drinking all the repressed anger was coming to the surface. Stuff that for years

Life in the balance

had been pushed down would emerge through the cathartic effect the drinking could have upon me. Even when still very young, at seventeen, whilst in Willemshaven, Germany during their 'beer festival,' I got so drunk; they had to keep me in sickbay for a day, due to the fact I was unconscious for so long. I had done things that offended people around me, and in fairness were 'out of character' but I was to an extent, when drinking, totally out of control. The Captain tried giving me a fatherly chat, but I was too proud to listen, so he gave me ten days punishment instead.

When I left that ship and joined a shore base for twelve months, I got very drunk. Someone decided to take advantage of the state I was in and I awoke to find myself in cells with a broken nose and very badly bruised ribs. I had been beaten quite badly and I had no recollection of it except odd flashbacks. I was in cells for the night, and sick bay for the best part of the day. I lost my two weeks leave because of that, which only resulted in me becoming even more offensive. I didn't realise the reputation I was gaining, and the effect that had upon those around you. I found that I became quite popular, because I could always be guaranteed to do something that would liven things up a little.

When under the influence I would be convinced that others were just spoiling for a fight. On my last ship, Sheila attended the commissioning weekend celebration. A young officer who had drank a half pint of lager and was quite 'flushed' was trying to be one of the boys. He put his arm around Sheila and said, "Who's this young filly then?" Actually, I was quite controlled due to the fact I had not had too much to drink by that time. However, I made it clear by my attitude and response to him that he was not welcome among us, and he left. My reward was to have an officer who made it his mission to seek me out for every rotten job he could find. I would continue this attitude even when home on leave. I

Life in the balance

couldn't see how embarrassing this could be for those around me.

I realised that I was fast becoming out of control as I contemplated taking drugs. Fortunately for me, apart from a minor experimentation, I chickened out and settled for what I thought then was a lesser evil. I stuck to the drinking. In the same way, when other guys would visit the brothels I would not. I was terrified of catching a sexually transmitted disease, so again, I would settle for what I then considered a lesser evil. I would go with my friends to sex shows, or watch blue movies, there was this camaraderie as we boosted one another's egos, and endorsed one another's behaviour. I did not see this as 'abusing myself,' I saw this as fun, and in my opinion at that time it gave me credibility with those around me.

Wearing a mask is very dangerous, for the image you seek to portray has to be lived up to. Most of the trouble I got into was as a direct result of trying to live up to something or someone I wasn't at heart. Consequently, I got into relationships that were simply to try and bolster my image, they rarely ever meant anything, and to my shame most of the girls I went out with I knew nothing about really (not even their names).

It was believed at one point that I had made a girlfriend pregnant, (because real men didn't use contraceptives). Fortunately, it was to prove that she wasn't. I knew she was using me, for whatever reasons, and if truth were said I was using her. My dad actually ended that relationship for me, he knew the risks we were taking, and was not happy about it.

I almost blew it on my first date with Sheila. I took her to a party at my Sisters home, and ended up getting into a scuffle with someone, convinced she would be impressed, and at a time I had been doing quite a bit of working out. I got hold of

Life in the balance

some chap in a corner and threatened to give him a good hiding. He was terrified I was going to hit him; I felt a sick kind of empowering through being able to better him. Needless to say, Sheila was not impressed, and I spent the next few weeks apologising to her by letter. I knew I had found the girl I would marry, and I never tried anything with her, I respected her and sincerely loved her, and was beginning to learn in a small way, that I could be as real as I was able to be with her.

What we believe are 'walls of protection' in fact can become so familiar to us that without realising it they actually do become a part of us. As a Christian all that happens is that these walls often remain, but they manifested differently – if you like, they take on a 'spiritual manifestation.' The need to control, the ability to manipulate circumstances and to an extent people, all these kind of personality traits and more revealed an immature kind of love, a love that stated, "I will love if." If I get my way all of the time?

Of course, I am sure we all know the story of Peter and how the Lord revealed to him that his love for the Lord, his loud, brash, naive affection for Jesus would have to be sifted and tested and shown for what it truly was. This was not a cruel act on the part of Jesus, but rather the process needed to give Peter what deep down he really wanted, a real uncompromising love for Jesus.

It took a 'crisis' to precipitate this real change in Peter, causing him to weep bitter tears, withdrawing to that which he was last secure in (i.e. fishing), yet clearly deep within he was at the least hoping for another chance, wanting to believe that perhaps he could still attain to his dream. Jesus of course had indicated that, when speaking prophetically of Peter's fall and subsequent restoration. Peter would not only recover himself, but would also strengthen the brethren around him.

Life in the balance

However, let's not make the mistake of thinking that this experience Peter went through was anything less than absolutely shattering for him. He probably really did think that he was this 'leader of men' the one who would so often speak out what he thought he really believed.

The truth is the potential was there, Jesus clearly saw it, however, he also saw the things that one day would need to be faced up to by Peter in order for him to become the great man of God he would be.

The storms that create the pressure or crisis needed to stop us continuing the way we are, do not in themselves provide the answers. When Peter faced the shattering experience of Jesus looking into his eyes, as the cock crowed, he entered a time in his life when all kinds of things could have potentially taken place. A storm of this kind is not intended to, as it were, keep us where we are, however, that is a great danger for some of us.

As someone has said, "God loves and accepts us as we are, but He loves us too much to leave us as we are." The valleys are never meant to become the graveyards. We all know and understand (in theory) that in fact the valley experiences are where the growing is taking place. However, we need to understand that there is a sense in which the choice is always before us.

Life in the balance

Chapter Five – Frozen in the storm

"Don't be afraid, do not despair, try and remember I'll always be there,
The waters are a'rising, the storm is at its worst,
The dam gates are a straining they're ready to burst,
Just keep your eyes on me and take a firm hold,
There's nothing that can break the gate of the fold.

Remember when, I came to you, I said I'd care for you I'd always come through,
And now the storm is at its head, I'm still here by your side,
Just lift your head and trust in me, my arms are open wide,
Run to me and see my words are true, my peace my love my life I gave for you.

Now take my hand, and stand up tall, the waters are a falling I've quietened down the storm,
It's time to make your stand for me, and show the world outside, the spirit that's within you is very much alive,
Then they will see the power that sets you free, as you take your walk of faith back home to me.

Song written during a storm D Crabb.

When I was in the Royal Navy, I spent quite a long period of time on fishery protection during what was referred to as the "Cod war." This was a strange time. Our job was to bring a level of protection to the trawler fleet, which was in dispute with Iceland over where they could and could not fish.

As a result, Iceland sent gunboats to basically harass the trawlers, and whenever an opportunity arose, cut their nets, which in fact was extremely dangerous.

Life in the balance

'Well thank goodness the Royal Navy was there.' (Hurrah!) We patrolled within the vicinity of the trawlers, and whenever gunboats appeared we would just get in the way of them, which inevitably involved us being rammed. When we were rammed, a great cheer would go up among the crew as it meant having to go back to port to be repaired.

We had our multi-million pound frigates, brimming with the latest technology and weapon systems. Yet, all we could do was either jeer at the gunboats, or throw the occasional potato when they got too close. We would end up getting rammed and holed, each side blaming the other for the incident.

When we eventually went back to Plymouth for major repairs, there were so many cod in the ships freezers that everyone had to take three or four home with them. They were wrapped in newspaper for us, and we put them up in the luggage racks. After a couple of hours, you can imagine the smell. Strangely enough no one seemed to want to share a compartment full of beer swilling sailors, and packages full of dead fish dangling from the luggage racks. When I arrived home, dad had those fish in the pan so fast, he was a great cook.

While in the Arctic Circle we often encountered very severe storms, which in fact were very frightening. It was almost impossible to get any sleep during these times, and all you could do was to get on your bunk, strap yourself down, get into a position that gave some comfort and try to sleep.

You know, when we encounter the storms of life that is often what we do. We adopt a certain position and seek to ride out that time in our lives. The trouble is when the storm ends we can still be frozen in a particular attitude.

Life in the balance

HMS Galatea (background), my second ship, about to be rammed by Gunboat Odin. We looked forward to these times as it meant going back to port for repairs, and hopefully some home leave.

Life in the balance

Gunboat Baldur crossing the bows of HMS Galatea in an attempt at making it appear we had rammed them.

Though we remained light-hearted during this time in Iceland, you can see from the damage sustained by the gunboat after being rammed by an angry trawler boat, that things did get quite dangerous. In fact, after this incident the gunboat threatened to open fire on the trawler, we were called to intervene.

It is entirely possible that we begin a process of analysis that really does not help us to enter into the freedom we long for. We adopt a position that we took up during a stormy time of our life, and therefore are not in a place where we can truly receive any kind of enlightenment at all.

For example, at the time we went through the prolonged period where everything we did seemed to go wrong, it seemed as though all we had was attacked, family members, our home and possessions it was a horrible time in our lives.
It culminated at a time when I felt I let not only myself down but more importantly those around me who I realise loved me very much. I experienced what I now understand to have been a complete 'burn out.'

Life in the balance

Being diagnosed by my GP as having 'reactive depression' further compounded what I saw as complete failure. I was required to take at least five weeks off, to attend regular counselling sessions, and even when I did return it was to a very different ministry. Those around me who loved me began making decisions that were to protect me, but I began to see them differently.

I felt as though I had failed, I was vulnerable, to an extent exposed to the judgement of others; it was to say the least uncomfortable. I adopted a position of self-protection and came dangerously close to shutting everyone out. I knew as a Pastor that people's perceptions about others often change when they have access to information that they may not have had previously.

I was very frightened. However, I began to realise that others did not see me as I thought they did. I had placed expectations upon myself that others never meant me to live up to. I also began to see that there were in fact a large number of folks who loved me for who I was, not merely what I thought I could do. The respect I received from people I never expected it from was amazing. The attitude seemed to be that they were blessed to have a pastor who was willing to be open and honest about where he was.

At that point I began to see it was time to get out of the position that somehow kept me in a storm that was no longer there. It was also time to get hold of what God was teaching me through all of this and seek further intimacy with Him.

Maintaining the kind of position that one takes while encountering the storms of life is at the least defensive, and at times causes you to see in an obtuse kind of way. I can recall feeling as though my hand was almost frozen to a sword; I saw

Life in the balance

all approaches to me as hostile. I expected nothing but problems. If someone asked to see me I would imagine all kinds of negative reasons for them wanting to speak to me.

I was unpleasant to live with. I avoided fellowship; shunning even those I previously enjoyed being with. Not realising I was further compounding things for they were now coming to the place where they assumed there were issues between us. One never sees clearly when isolated.

I wanted to be able to be vulnerable again, yet at the same time doubted the motivations of those around me. I began to become quite cynical about human nature, and even Christianity. Not realising that this attitude was causing me to live under a spirit of fear. Once again, I initiated a search for a way out. Perhaps I was in the wrong ministry? Maybe it was time to get out of ministry altogether and seek secular employment?

I could not see that the things that I considered to be safety harnesses were in fact now the very things that were restricting me, holding me back, and stopping me from walking free from the storm. I needed intimacy with Father, and I also needed fellowship with those who deep down I knew loved me. They were distressed and upset and definitely as confused as I was over the things that had taken place in my life. They simply wanted me to be well, and I underestimated the effect that the whole experience had upon them.

These walls were going to have to come down, and I was the one who was going to have to bring them down, before Father needed to take a hand in the matter. One thing that I learnt from my storm experiences in the Navy was that to remain in a storm for a prolonged period would definitely cause sickness. However, a positive benefit from riding out the storms was that eventually you gained what we referred to as 'sea legs.'

Life in the balance

I remember one guy who was used to the storms and had reached a place where the constant heaving and throwing of the ship no longer affected his sense of equilibrium. He would often come into the mess deck and with a great sense of sadistic pleasure proceed to open a jar of pickled onions. His generosity was astounding; he made sure not one single person missed out as he waved the jar ceremoniously under our noses.

I suppose in some kind of cruel way he helped. If there had been anything of your stomach contents left at that time, this was sure to bring them forth, usually in an embarrassing way. That's the trouble with storms isn't it? Their timing, and the fact that you can, to an extent, be at the mercy of them. If you had a friend of course you could guarantee they would be there for you, holding the bucket, maintaining to a degree your dignity.

That is providing you have not isolated yourself by then. The analogy there is clear I would hope. You see the storms can cause us, as I have said already, to become so defensive and unpleasant that when they reach their head, and we really need someone, our reactions can be the very things that ensure we are alone.

I wonder. Have you yet realised that perhaps the storm is actually over? Constantly reliving it, revising it, analysing it will not help you be free from it. There has to be an acceptance of it. For whatever reason the Lord allowed it, but there has to be a time you decide to walk through it.

Life in the balance

Taken from the bridge of HMS Galatea during a bad storm, whilst on fishery protection. The ship sustained quite a lot of damage to the superstructure during this particular storm.

It is when we decide to do that our eyes are opened in all kinds of ways. Sometimes in His grace the Lord allows us a glimpse as to the why? Other times we see the where? Alternatively, we see the what? I personally believe the main common denominator in it all is that we arrive at a place called 'enlightenment.' Before arrival we need to be stripped of our clothes of sickness, pride, sin and the like.

I would add regarding storms; our experience during 'stormy seasons' has often been a mixture of, humanly speaking, highs and lows. The trouble is, what we often consider to be a low, could in fact prove to be a growth time. And what we consider a high point, nothing more than an emotional catharsis. Let me illustrate what I mean.

When in a storm on a ship, it was always fun timing your ascent on a ladder when the ship was in the process of plummeting down from the crest of a wave. For a matter of a few short seconds it was as though you were almost

Life in the balance

weightless. So, the ships course was downward whereas your course was upward. However, when the ship was climbing a wave it was as though you had gained several stones in weight. The simple point in all of this is that things are not always what they appear to be. God's idea of a blessing could appear as something entirely different to us. And our idea of blessing could be seen as entirely different to God's.

Life in the balance

Chapter Six - The Desert of no Short Cuts

"In a desert land he found him, in a barren and howling waste. He shielded him and cared for him; he guarded him as the apple of his eye." Deut 32:10

The temptation in walking out of an attitude that one has taken, as the result of a storm is to think that we just come right on out straight into great blessing. I recall a stormy incident in the life of Moses. He was to discover a principle that I have needed to discover over and over again. Spiritual ends are never achieved by carnal means. I heard a preacher once put it this way, "When the self life finally sits down, the well of a new life lies near."

Moses was to learn this principle, and the process was initiated through failure. Psalm 119:67 says, "Before I was afflicted I went astray, but now I keep your word." V71-72 says, "It was good for me to be afflicted so that I might learn your decrees. The law from your mouth is more precious to me than thousands of pieces of silver and gold."

Whenever we experience failure it causes us to want to lead an obedient life, and helps to build a teachable spirit within us.

Once again, I will quote one of my favourite people Winston Churchill who said, "Success is the moving from one failure to another with no loss of enthusiasm."

I have found that when I have met with people who I know truly hear from the Holy Spirit and are sensitive to Him, they have their scars, or limps, they can tell you of the times they needed to be broken, the humbling process that has gone on in

Life in the balance

their lives, the painful lessons at times they have learnt through trying to achieve a spiritual end through carnal means.

During a time in the life of Moses when he had gone out to where his own people were, after witnessing the beating of one of his people by an Egyptian, he decided to take matters into his own hands. His solution was to kill the Egyptian and bury him in the sand. The trouble was he left a big toe protruding and consequently was found out. He also experienced a level of rejection from his own people, and so he fled until he came to a place called Midian, and there we find him sitting by a well.

Something I have discovered about myself is my ability to put up with pressure, there lay my problem, it meant that I had to come to a place where I could no longer put up with it, in fact, where I broke embarrassingly so. A body was Moses point of exposure, what is yours? There is a huge difference between coping with pressure, and putting up with pressure.

Here we have Moses at a time in his life when he has realised his true heritage, shows a real concern for his people and a desire rises within him. A noble desire without doubt, the mistake being he thinks he can do something about it in his own strength. Some commentators believe that Moses knew nothing of the call of God on his life until the burning bush. I believe that scripture implies he had some idea but that he perhaps failed in seeking God about it.

Well here he is now enrolled in Gods training school. Now I attended Bible school at Capel, Surrey. Amid beautiful grounds, I lived in a fairly comfortable dormitory, eating well, and basically enjoying the favour of the Lord. However, Gods training schools can be somewhat different. In this instance the location is a wilderness, some spend a few months, some a few years – Moses was to spend 40 years. In fact, the Hebrew

Life in the balance

word for desert is 'midbaar' from the root word 'dahbaar' meaning 'to speak.'

Obviously, the desert experience is not the place that you find Christians volunteering to go to, however it is the place that at times we need to be in order to hear from the Lord.

Many do not want to hear about the desert because it is so very different from our western culture and mindset. We live in a world of noise, mobile phones, stereo's, tv's and so on. The desert is all about loneliness, solitude, quiet. Living in a world of noise to an extent cuts you off from your real self – who you really are before the Lord. We so often blank out much of what God wants to communicate to us by keeping busy, or filling our lives with noise.

The wilderness changes all that. We get stripped of all our comforts, all the things we were convinced we so desperately needed. It becomes very quiet. The desert can be representative of all kinds of experiences – suffering, a boring job, failure in some area, it could be all manner of things that act almost like a doorway, bringing you into a desert like state. The emotions you can experience are loneliness, feeling you've been shelved, barrenness, confusion and almost in every case an extreme sense of a loss of confidence.

In our passage in Deuteronomy it is described as a howling waste. My howling waste may be completely different to another's, for God knows exactly the context that is needed to bring me to a place of brokenness. Strangely enough Moses was in mid-life, we often laugh about these kinds of things but it is really no joke when you start to ask questions like; Where am I going? What am I doing? Where will I end up?

I want to encourage you right away from this one verse in Deut' for we are told four very important things. In this

Life in the balance

howling waste we are in he will **find** us, secondly, we will be **shielded** by Him, thirdly we will be **cared** for, and fourthly we will be **guarded** (as the apple of his eye). If we really accept this and believe it we couldn't be in a better place, could we? It all points to an encounter, which is Gods greatest form of blessing.

My friend, whatever happened to bring you to your howling waste, whichever doorway if you like that you entered in by is nowhere near as important as, what does God want to say to me? What is He saying to me?

There have been and still are times in my walk when God says to me, "Be still and sit and listen," and I obey. However, there are things that drive me at times, guilt, insecurities, unreal expectations, misguided loyalty to something or someone and so on. These are the things that I have been saying need to be faced up to, and it is in this place that the Lord will help us to see.

Sometimes leaders find it difficult to enter into this quiet place, to be vulnerable, open and transparent. This is because sometimes they have been taken advantage of during a time of vulnerability which has mistakenly been misinterpreted as weakness. Moses of course we are told was the meekest man on the face of the earth, yet he was not weak. Sometimes this is one of the very reasons the Lord needs to take his servant aside, to heal them of the abuses they have suffered at the hands of those they are serving.

One other thing to mention about the wilderness, especially within the context of leaders, and that is the lesson of obscurity. Verse 12 of Deuteronomy 32 says, "The Lord alone led him; no foreign God was with him."

Life in the balance

Most of us if we are honest like to think that we are being led by the Lord alone. However, if we were to be totally honest and humble we would see that at times there are many other things involved. Comfort, finance, self-motivations, scheming, selfish desire such as envy or greed, the lust for success. Then perhaps some of the outer pressures such as peer pressure, media pressure all the plethora of noise this world gives off.

But for the leader there are going to be times when God takes him aside for further lessons in being led by God and God alone. I had a lesson in being alone with God, when in 1993 I was asked to go to Tanzania, alone, for a period of two months. I was to teach in the Bible School. Because I was used to travelling I thought I would find this relatively easy, however I was in for a shock.

The whole experience challenged me in a way that I had not anticipated. I truly did experience God in a whole new way. The fact was I was cut off from my culture; I had no one with me so effectively I was without friends. The missionaries in Tanzania at that time were on furlough. I lived in an African out house, and ate very frugally. Looking back, I can see the incredible benefits I experienced at that time, however, at the time it was one of the most challenging things I had ever done.

Moses had forty years of obscurity. I have been in ministry now for a mere fifteen years. I would hardly say I live a life of obscurity. Some would consider the church I pastor reasonably successful, but we are talking about character here not mere success in ministry. God will not hurry the lessons of character.

Well, in Exodus 2:11-15 we see that Moses arrives in Midian where we are told he sits down by a well. Moses sits at last, no longer running, and he is right next to a well where he can be refreshed.

Life in the balance

(Song/D Crabb)

When everything is dark around me, and my faith is down,
Even as I call your name, it doesn't feel like you're around,
When the road I take seems long and hard, and my worries weigh me down,
I come aside, no longer hide, listening for your voice inside,
Lord I really need to hear today.

The valley's getting deeper still, Oh Lord I'm so afraid,
My tendency's to turn and run, or pretend I have it made,
Then when you speak the words you say, they really break my heart,
I turn around, there's holy ground, 'cause in my weakness your grace I've found,
Lord I'm lost for words what can I say?

You're the Lord who searches hearts, the secrets of the mind,
And only you can know the things, that cause me to try and find,
The peace I'll only find in you, the joy of new life known,
I have to learn, my sin must burn, the love you give I cannot earn,
Lord keep me in your Eternal arms.

To look within and face my sins, to grieve then turn away,
To look upon the face of Him, who came for us, and paid,
That's all you ever ask of me, to trust and to obey,
So I turn around, there's holy ground, 'cause in my weakness your grace I've found,
Lord I'm lost for words what can I say?

Life in the balance

Chapter seven –Quiet waters

"He leads me beside quiet waters, He restores my soul." Psalm 23

I wonder after his journey in the wilderness and his subsequent arrival at Midian what the first thoughts of Moses were? Surely, he would be Hungry, Thirsty, it must have been some journey? For Elijah on the run the same thing applied, food and drink, for there was another journey of discovery ahead of him.

Psalm 23 has to be probably the most loved and well-known Psalm in scripture. I always say when speaking from this passage that it is all about He and Me! Many times, I have heard people say, "We are human beings not human doings."

You know Psalm 84 talks about going through a place of dryness, in fact a valley called 'Baca' that is a place of weeping. There is much in that Psalm, and a lot about springs of water, those that are created by us in Christ, and those that come sovereignly from the Lord.

Remember the positions we often take as a result of being in the storm? Well, there is a sanctuary that we can withdraw to if we could but see it, and recognise that there is not only a sheltering place, but also a place of refreshment and restoration. What will it cost you may ask? The same it cost Moses, Sitting down!

When I think of some of the prayers I have made, I am forced to ask myself a most probing question. Am I really prepared for God to answer my prayers? Melt me? Mould me? Fill me?

Life in the balance

Make me willing to be willing? Search me and know me? I wonder, how many reading this, have prayed similar prayers?

For God to answer, will certainly require us to 'get down' or to 'sit down' or to 'be still,' basically to humble ourselves. What are the questions we are really asking? Some pray simply for God to make them successful, many Pastors pray for God to bless their Church (I am learning actually it's Gods church), everyone agrees that we must pray, but not many seem to think that the answers to those prayers apply to them as individuals.

"If my people, who are called by my name, will humble themselves and pray and seek my face and turn from their wicked ways, then will I hear from heaven and will forgive their sin and heal their land." 2 Chron 7:14

I have made it clear that this book is not written by someone who thinks he has all the answers, rather from someone who is in the humbling position of being taught at the time of writing. What can often keep you humble is the fact that the growth process can be such an ugly thing. It requires great patience on the part of all. We can end up in conflict with God, with ourselves and with others. And when things get 'ugly' it can often be at the price of relationships.

During these past few years of what seems to have been a constant state of learning and re-learning the Lord has graciously brought me to a well of refreshment, in fact more than that, a quiet stream of Grace and favour. I have come to refer to these times as 'Quiet waters.'

I cannot help but think of that proud warrior Naaman who was told by the prophet that in order for him to receive his healing he must dip himself in the Jordan river seven times. I know we

Life in the balance

have all heard the sermon, however, I would often imagine him as he eventually humbled himself to the task.

Just imagine with me for a moment. Stripping off his armour, even his clothing perhaps, going into that river as naked as the day he was born, and as we know eventually coming out totally cleansed and healed. I would often wonder to myself, I wonder what Naaman would have done if someone had witnessed this act of humility and perhaps said something inappropriate?

You see there are times in my walk that I have longed, desired for a sense of intimacy with the Lord that will require me to be stripped of everything. There is a fear in being stripped isn't there? That once we are naked everyone could potentially see us for who and what we really are. All that perhaps had been cleverly covered over by our armour is suddenly exposed.

How vulnerable that makes us, how open to criticism and wounding. We can believe that we must appear so ugly to those around us, when in fact the opposite is more often the case.

It can be very difficult for those in the body of Christ to be completely open and transparent. But I wonder if we ever stop to consider how difficult it can also be for those in leadership or positions that give them a very public platform. No matter how secure we like to think we are, we all need a level of protection when entering a time, or season in our lives where the Lord requires us to join Him at the waters.

Writing this book has been, to say the least, challenging. It has meant being willing to share perhaps some of the less flattering aspects of one's life, to allow others in. But I have discovered that it has acted like a catalyst in having access to

Life in the balance

the lives of others who are fellow pilgrims, seeking the way through.

I believe that if Naamans servant had used this opportunity to mock him, or the like, Naaman would have almost certainly have taken his head off. I realise I may be accused of taking a lot of licence here, but is it any wonder when someone dares to become vulnerable, and perhaps lays everything down to enter the quiet waters, that they become so distressed, even cynical, when others use it as an opportunity to do a bit of analysing, or indeed a chance to keep you in your place as they see it.

This is a great danger when we seek to move alongside someone. We can be so quick to analyse, give our diagnosis, and then prognosticate as to what we think that person's problem is. Constantly analysing people, or even diagnosing their problems leads only to inertia. Criticism at this point can be very dangerous; do not be surprised if your head is bitten off if you dare to be too analytical with a vulnerable one.

The whole purpose of coming to the waters is to be restored, refreshed, and renewed in His presence. It is to this quiet place that the Great Shepherd longs to bring us, intimacy with Him is what we so often need. "Be still and know that I am God."
Not be still in order for everyone to analyse you. Or, be still so that we can tie you down and ensure you do not get up again.

Every creature has the need for water, and the way that is expressed is through thirsting. In the same way that our physical bodies have need for water, so also our souls have need for the water of the Spirit of the Eternal God. We can only truly be satisfied when our capacity for the spirit of God is fully quenched by drinking from Him. Jesus says, "Blessed are they who hunger and thirst after righteousness: for they shall be filled." Matthew 5:6

Life in the balance

You know, ideally, church should be the place where we can be completely open, vulnerable, and receptive to all that God wants for us. Sadly, that is not always the case, particularly for leaders. When we willingly decide to strip ourselves of anything that encumbers us, especially the masks and defence mechanisms we use, the barriers we erect to keep ourselves as we see it, secure.

HEB 12:1 "Therefore, since we are surrounded by such a great cloud of witnesses, let us throw off everything that hinders and the sin that so easily entangles, and let us run with perseverance the race marked out for us. Let us fix our eyes on Jesus, the author and perfecter of our faith, who for the joy set before him endured the cross, scorning its shame, and sat down at the right hand of the throne of God. Consider him who endured such opposition from men, so that you will not grow weary and lose heart."

Sheila and I had the privilege of going on sabbatical a number of years ago. We chose 'Church on the Way' in California as a place we would love to experience. I was struck by the open fellowship the men in particular seemed to enjoy. Confessing their faults, sins, and weaknesses, and praying with sincerity of heart. It seemed there was a genuine humbling towards one another.

It is right and proper that we are willing to strip ourselves, especially from the wrong form of armour, ie, that which we create ourselves. There is an occasion when armour is removed from a man in scripture that is very perturbing and should act as a warning to us all.

King Saul had his armour removed from his body, as he lay dead! His body was defiled and pinned to a wall for all his enemies to gloat over. I wonder, how many can you think of

Life in the balance

who sought to bypass the yoke of conviction, and ended up spiritually impoverished?

The purpose of God in bringing us to the quiet waters is to restore, refresh, renew. The question is, will we be lead to the waters? And what about the stripping away? Maybe we are afraid, perhaps in a time of vulnerability you have experienced those who would take advantage of such times.

Well, you are in good company. Our Lord made Himself completely vulnerable for us, it is entirely possible that at times we may enter into His sufferings. But it is far better to be led to the quiet waters than for us to seek waters ourselves, thirsting can cause you to settle for what turns out to be a 'mirage.' In the next chapter I want to look at another word that begins with 'R.' Recreation.

(Song/D Crabb)

There's a place I love to go, there's a God who loves us so,
He'll take you in, if you'll take His hand,
Don't be afraid, there's no sinking sand.
There's a love that's real and pure, there's a joy a peace so sure,
It's yours to know, it's yours to share,
Just trust in Him and He'll take you there,

Because He loves you, He loves you don't you know?
Yes He loves you.........

Life in the balance

Chapter eight – Beware the polluted holes

We need to be led by the Lord to the quiet waters, if we are not led it is entirely possible that we settle for water that is actually polluted. Some make the mistake of thinking during their thirsting that they need recreation. Re-creation perhaps, but recreation can be tantamount to settling for polluted water. Allow me to quote C H Spurgeon, "The yoke of censure is an irksome one, but it prepares a man for future honour. He is not fit to be a leader who has not run the gauntlet of contempt. Praise intoxicates if it not be preceded by abuse. Men who rise to eminence without a struggle usually fall into dishonour. The yoke of affliction, disappointment, and excessive labour is by no means to be sought for; but when the Lord lays it on us in our youth it frequently develops a character which glorifies God and blesses the church." Unquote.

In the time that we are really thirsting we need to ensure we are properly focussed. I say that because it is so easy to go chasing after what turns out to be a 'mirage.' Again, within the whole context of this book, we are talking about a possible scenario where someone refuses to face up to a less flattering aspect of their character that God perhaps wants to deal with.

The process that the Lord initiates in our life is just too painful, therefore we take a detour that seems to offer the same results, yet comes at a lower price. I once heard this referred to as, "achieving a legitimate end by using illegitimate means." That of course was how the devil tempted our Lord Himself.

I began to see how at times in my own life I was pursuing after, what resulted in being, dirty or polluted water. But also, how this attitude could transpose into how I was dealing with those I was called to shepherd.

Life in the balance

For example; the only way a person will ever be truly born again is when they experience the conviction of the Holy Spirit, confess their sin, repent and have faith in Christ Jesus, receive His forgiveness and cleansing, and begin to follow His leading. "It is good for a man that he bear the yoke in his youth." Lam 3:27 It is not good that we merely panic when convicted by the Holy Spirit and seek our own way, we must allow the work of conviction to run its whole course, which leads us to confession and repentance and true faith in Christ Jesus.

As an under shepherd I have had to learn the painful lesson of not falling into the temptation of trying to make things easier for people. If I interfere in the processes of God I will only ever lead people to ditches or potholes of pollution. Those who have learnt to bear the reproach of the cross will reach the quiet waters of God.

LA 2:14 The visions of your prophets were false and worthless; they did not expose your sin to ward off your captivity.

We need to beware the Christ complex, meaning, that desire within us to continually want to save people as it were. In fact leaders who are this way inclined often do more harm than good. It can encourage weakness in people.

As I read and meditated in Psalm 23 one day, I felt the Lord really speak to me and cause me to again understand the intimacy of His wonderful word. "He makes ME lie down," "He leads ME," just look for yourself at all the times the Psalmist uses such personal terms. Me, I, My. There are some things that we all must experience for ourselves, and at times I could see I was getting in the way.

Life in the balance

There are times during our wanderings that we have to be allowed to really thirst. In order that our thirst causes us to call upon the only one who can truly satisfy. For some, who are perhaps occasionally more stubborn than others, (like me), this has meant having the occasional draught of dirty water. The effect this has of course is to make us sick. So sick, as to drive us harder towards the sweet waters that only Jesus provides.

"Even though we speak like this, dear friends, we are confident of better things in your case--things that accompany salvation. God is not unjust; he will not forget your work and the love you have shown him as you have helped his people and continue to help them. We want each of you to show this same diligence to the very end, in order to make your hope sure. We do not want you to become lazy,
but to imitate those who through faith and patience inherit what has been promised." Heb 6:9

This passage comes after a very difficult one, but let me assure you. Whilst you are still thirsting for those waters there is hope!

You know it is entirely possible that we begin to settle for 'lesser things,' or that in fact we become lazy in the things of God. Very often, when experiencing times of great difficulty, stress or wilderness we are tempted into seeking other forms of recreation. We fail to see how these things are mere distractions at times, and actually hinder us from finding the 'quiet waters,' those that will truly re-create us.

On a more dangerous note, it can be while on a quest for recreation that we fall into more sinister things. Areas of sin, where we become enticed, because of laziness in spirit, and consequently find ourselves in a kind of stupor. In these times it is possible that we could end up doing a lot of harm to ourselves. Consider King David strolling the palace balcony,

Life in the balance

drawn into a voyeuristic fantasy, which eventually ends up with him seeking to turn that fantasy into reality, with disastrous consequences.

This can be likened to sitting in front of the TV set flicking through the channels, (what is it we are looking for?). It can also be likened to surfing the net almost absentmindedly. My own conviction is that the internet is a dangerous place, many Godly people are becoming ensnared. In fact, internet pornography is fast becoming predatory in its attempts to lure people in. I have met a number of Church leaders who have been purposely sent e-mails with attachments that they have opened, and as a result exposed their souls to things that have an incredible effect.

I believe one of the finest tools any Christian can put on their computer is good 'filtering software,' to ensure you are not exposed to some of the filth currently so easily available.

The previous General Superintendant of the Elim Church, Rev John Glass has referred to the danger of drinking from polluted streams. What are these polluted streams? Well they can also be things that on the surface may not seem 'evil' or even 'wrong' in themselves. But they can be the very distractions that we do not need at that time in our life, that result in us failing to experience the 'quiet waters' where our Father wants to meet with us.

There are 'better things' – things that 'accompany salvation.' The warning in Hebrews is concerning laziness. Friends let us not be deceived here. Perhaps you are working very hard, and being called lazy would be incredibly insulting. But there are times we need to ask ourselves, "What am I busy in?" TV? Computer? Movies? I am not suggesting that these things in themselves are terribly evil, but what is this time in your life? Where are you at the moment? Are any of these things

Life in the balance

hindering you from finding the quiet waters? As my Pastor once said, "If you are too busy for God then you are too busy."

We all know I am sure the teaching on the 'seasons' in our lives. "A time for everything." There are times for recreation, chilling out, enjoying ourselves, but there is also a time to 'seek the Lord.' "He makes me lie down" in those times of lying down I have heard the word of God. "He leads me beside still waters" in those times I am restored. "He guides me in paths of righteousness" in those times I have come forth, changed, renewed, others have seen what God has done in me.

Would you really want to miss all of that? For what? A programme on tv, some amusement on the internet? The latest movies that you just have to see? When just entering into a 'quiet moment' with the Lord may have brought you so much. His revelatory word, His restoring presence, a changed life.

During my depression I entered, for a time, what I can only refer to as a place of utter desolation. I could see nothing in terms of my future. My life seemed to a certain extent be out of control, a roller coaster of emotions. Even this can be likened to drinking from pollution. In this very vulnerable state the enemy of our souls will also take a hand, this is when he will attack. However, when the enemy presses in like a flood the Lord will raise up a banner against him. "But for those who fear you, you have raised a banner to be unfurled against the bow" Psa 60:4

There is always a positive to all the negatives that seem to come against us. As I began to question the questions they could not help but give themselves away. "Why are you downcast oh my soul?" Doubt the doubts? Question the questions? God can and will reveal to you the areas that are 'magnified' during the season of desolation.

Life in the balance

In my case the attacks persisted for a season. Someone who was very close to me, literally a day after my father died decided this was the time I needed to hear a scripture. "We were with child, we writhed in pain, but we gave birth to wind. We have not brought salvation to the earth; we have not given birth to people of the world." Isa 26:18

Their conclusion was that this was what had happened, in their opinion, concerning my spiritual vision, my hopes and dreams. I was so distressed in spirit at the time that I simply agreed with them. I knew that they meant well, I did not, and do not even now doubt their motive, but it wasn't doing me any good at all.

On arrival at my home the Lord began to speak to me. First of all, He reminded me of the importance of examining all of the surrounding verses to His word, and also what a mistake it is to take scripture out of context to use as a pretext to say what we believe is true. "But your dead will live; their bodies will rise.You who dwell in the dust, wake up and shout for joy". Isa 26:19

The next thing the Lord did was to remind me of all the great heroes of faith mentioned in Hebrews 11. "All these people were still living by faith when they died. They did not receive the things promised; they only saw them and welcomed them from a distance" Heb 11:13.

Strange how things began to appear differently. Then I received from the Lord the kick I needed.

"So, do not throw away your confidence; it will be richly rewarded. You need to persevere so that when you have done the will of God, you will receive what he has promised. For in just a very little while,

Life in the balance

"He who is coming will come and will not delay. But my righteous one will live by faith. And if he shrinks back, I will not be pleased with him." But we are not of those who shrink back and are destroyed, but of those who believe and are saved. Now faith is being sure of what we hope for and certain of what we do not see. This is what the ancients were commended for". Heb 10:35-11:2

I just knew that I was now drinking from the 'sweet waters.' I was in the quiet place, his word came to me again in revelation, I was restored, and I came forth in new faith. In fact after visiting a senior colleague, pastor George Canty, I saw the fulfillment of a prophetic word he spoke over me, "The word will come to you again."

My friend, what are you drinking in? What are you soaking up? Is it dirty polluted water? You know the Lord reminded me once again that I am His precious child who is growing still.

I remember when I was very young I used to get a lot of pains in my legs. My Grandmother used to say to me, "Don't worry they're just growing pains." Growing up can be painful. I remember John Glass speaking over my life on one occasion. He said, "David, God has a bigger jacket for you to wear. He is growing you into it."

When God is working and growing us in the process, we need a new wineskin to contain the new growth. Note how Wineskin is spelt, not Whineskin. Sometimes, in biblical times a wineskin would become dry, even cracked, and rather than dispose of it they would take them down to the river and leave them there to soak. Soaked wineskins become more flexible, durable and ultimately developable – this all involves change.

Life in the balance

I was so blessed to get a word like that. Let's be honest, how many of us truthfully when we go out for prayer want God to give the man of God a nice word for us? Something encouraging, please Lord. I loved the part about the bigger jacket, for it seemed to suggest something good, however the bit about, growing into it was not as encouraging.

From a Father to a son.(D Crabb/song)
There's always pain, there's always tears,
At times there's doubt, sometimes there are fears,
Sometimes you feel you can't go on, you won't admit 'cause they say it's wrong,
But there's one thing you ought to know, from a Father to his son, these things you see, make you like me, you're growing my son.

The day I called and you came to me,
What did I say? What did you see?
Was it not truth I gave to you?
It set you free you were born anew,
Yet times you've strayed and walked away, despite the words I gave, a lesson learnt at times brings pain – you're growing my son.

Growing pains are often hard to bear, especially with an enemy so near,
But like a parent that watches tends and cares, I won't let you go there's nothing you need fear!

So when there's pain, when you're crying tears,
Deny the doubts, fight back the fears,
Then lift your head and call to me,
For I will answer, I'll set you free,
And be encouraged do not despair, it's fairly plain to see,
A growing heart can take more seed, you're growing, you're growing my son.

Life in the balance

Chapter Nine Don't Wail, Travail

"In the six hundredth year of Noah's life, on the seventeenth day of the second month--on that day all the springs of the great deep burst forth, and the floodgates of the heavens were opened. And rain fell on the earth forty days and forty nights." Gen 7:11-12

We have seen how pressure can magnify. We need to understand that when God allows tests it is in order to bring out the best in us. Temptations of course are designed to bring out the worst; it is best not to confuse the two. God is good all the time; all the time God is good. He has His own agenda, but be sure of this much, it is to bring forth His glory every time.

We are seeing I am sure that we are a work in progress. I can recall when first ministering in a church on some of the things mentioned in this book, a lady approaching me to tell me (quite enthusiastically) that she was praying Psalm 139 over her life. Especially the part, "Search me, know me, test me," later, it seemed as though every possible problem came upon her – "Suddenly."

I am discovering that there is an eternity of difference between the revelations of God, as opposed to God actually explaining Himself. God reveals Himself to us in so many different ways, but there is not necessarily an explanation. Some things, for some reason He withholds, sometimes it would seem almost tantalisingly.

There are some things going on within us that have to be brought to birth, and instead of moaning and groaning about our situations, sometimes we need to begin travailing in order

Life in the balance

to bring to birth that which in essence is completed within us but needs to be expressed in an outward way.

You know delivery is not always a pleasant experience. I would feel far from qualified to speak about delivery within the context of mid-wifery. My knowledge is very limited in that area, I could only speak as a 'dad' my wife would know all about the pain of course. The only pain I could speak of was her nails in my arm etc.

Now to travail means literally, 'to labour or toil,' which of course, implies effort?

There have been times in my ministry that I have been, to an extent, criticised because of bringing myself under pressure with regards to my spiritual growth. I am sure that those gentle criticisms have an element of truth about them. However, as someone once said, "I would rather be wrong trying to be right, than safe." Another once said, "you cannot make a splash without going overboard."

The truism in all of this is that some things in God require effort on our part. God has done all that is necessary within us. Gestation has run its course, but the birthing of that which is within will require cooperation. Of course, there is considerable risk at this point (birthing), and I am afraid to say that the whole birthing process can often be most undignified. I am sure I have no need to explain further.

You see, the whole process of following Jesus cannot be for those who fear making mistakes, getting it wrong, or simply need to constantly be in the right in order to feel accepted. Our salvation began with a confession that in fact we were totally wrong! Jesus said, "It is not the healthy who need a doctor, but the sick."

Life in the balance

Following Jesus is almost impossible for anyone who wants to keep hold of his or her dignity at all times. Those who are not willing in a sense to share their own weakness and require to constantly be in control, or in a superior place will never bring anything to birth.

It is virtually impossible to have a 'moment in God' without it involving all of you. And at times it is the fear of losing dignity that hinders us receiving our moment. Real change always involves pressure, and will certainly mean travailing.

God will always bring to completion that which He has started in our lives, sometimes, even at our request through prayer. We ask God to do things; it doesn't happen immediately; therefore, we wrongly assume God has not answered the prayer.

Actually, many times He has answered with a seed, conception, then gestation takes place, and suddenly the pressure of contractions begin, and a travailing, needs to take place as we realise, 'this is my moment.'

"Do I bring to the moment of birth and not give delivery?" says the LORD. "Do I close up the womb when I bring to delivery?" says your God." Isa 66:9

If we refuse to cooperate with God at this point, we could be facing an abortion simply because we closed up, backed off, failed to realise that this in fact was our moment in God.

Let me point out one or two obvious things concerning the whole process of delivering a baby. First of all, there is a total loss of dignity for the one giving birth. Others see parts of you; you would prefer were left covered up. The spiritual point there is obvious. There is intense pain and incredible effort. There has to be faith in those who are attending your birth, the

Life in the balance

midwife, doctor perhaps, and encourager. One thing is for sure; once birthing has started there is no going back.

I remember when Sheila had our first child. It was a time when we were completely in the hands of those who knew what they were doing. It was in some ways a discomfiting experience to be so dependent on others.

I know there have been times in my own life, when there was a 'birthing moment,' and because of fear of one kind or another, I missed it. When I was a young Christian this was once manifested through me asking God to give me spiritual gifts.

He answered that prayer immediately, however, it was about three weeks later that He gave me what I now realise was a prophetic utterance for the Church. I chickened out, and realised afterwards that I had literally aborted something precious. Fortunately, He is the God who gives us more than one chance.

We tell Non-Christians in our meetings, 'just come as you are,' that is true, however, we also need to make sure they understand that although God is not judging us for who we are, there are times He will judge us for refusing to become what He intends us to be.

Change, or the willingness to change is not a matter of us trying to 'prove' something; it is a matter of being willing to 'improve.' The verse we have in Genesis speaks of the waters in the deep breaking forth before the waters from heaven come. Before a real birth takes place there is a breaking within us (perhaps a little like the breaking of a woman's waters).

Brokenness has to come before birthing can take place. Most of the breaking points in my life have been preceded by some

Life in the balance

kind of crisis. Charles Finney was asked to define revival, his response was, "A renewed time of real obedience to God," the implication was that it was his belief that we need to be broken regularly before God.

In our complete arrogance we always assume that we are aware of where our need for change is. We think that it is only within the arena of the conscious mind that God is at work. I never dreamt for a moment that God would deal with me in some of the recent areas He has worked in; the whole process has been most embarrassing and painful.

There have been times in my life where I have had to acknowledge that I have operated in half-truths. I have learnt that half a truth is a whole lie. I used to think I must be the only Christian Pastor who has this sin, until I started to listen to some of the claims being made over meetings and the like. You see, even an exaggeration is a total lie! Here's the sting, **you only get credit for the lie.**

There is only one way to deal with that – confess it, agree with God, move outside your dignity and repent. This whole subject of moving beyond our dignity has to go further than whether or not we dance in Church, or experience any other manifestation of Praise and Worship. It has to do with us!

Fundamentalists are often put off concerning any teaching about moving beyond our dignity, for they assume that it is going to be limited to whether or not we speak in tongues or manifest in other ways.

I heard an interesting definition of fundamentalism recently – 'No fun, mainly dumb and certainly mental.' That description needs to be narrowed down a great deal. You can love the word of God, be in awe of it, believe it to be the most

Life in the balance

important thing, yet totally miss its point because of refusing to move beyond one's own safety zone.

There are so many frustrated Christians in our churches today who are still wailing while they wait for God to do something. Often the truth is that He has already answered the prayers (sometimes even before they have been uttered), but His people are avoiding the travailing process to bring to birth what God has done.

Yet this is what Holiness is all about, completeness, wholeness that we are moving toward, that is Gods desire. Some limit holiness to mean, "cut it out or I'll kill you."

If you want to see what you have hoped, or longed for the first thing you have to do is believe it. If you believe you will see, not, see it first then believe.

Moving beyond your dignity could involve tears, it will certainly involve becoming childlike once again. I have discovered that being a Pastor should never mean I cannot be childlike with my Father, in fact recently I have learnt to actually call upon Him again as daddy, Father.

Life in the balance

(Song/D Crabb)
Blinded by the feeling that I've got to be the man, haunted by the lie that says you wouldn't understand,
Walking down the roads built on failure, fear and doubt, looking out never looking in, feeling I'm the one without.

Then after I have fallen down, I see your love filled hand, reaching in and touching all I thought I'd left behind,
I realise with some surprise the work you had begun, must finish all that you intend for me to still become.

Eyes that had grown scales have now been opened up again, I see you in a different light, set free from guilt and shame,
Within that safe protective love, that tells me do not fear, I stand once more not weak but strong and know that you are near.

So, Father me, yes father me, I'll no longer be ashamed, to let the tears flow down my face, to be a child again,
I'll walk once more within your love, certain and assured, I'll free the child that's here in me, and live my life restored.

I understand that in your hand there's nothing I need dread, my heart's healed long before I hear the words inside my head,
This isn't masochistic, this isn't playing games, for only you discern the heart, it's there that you will reign.

So, Father me, please Father me, I'm so tired of being cold, restore to me my child like trust that once dare not unfold,
And all that once was hurt or used, so damaged insecure, as I am healed you'll give me back my innocence and more.

Life in the balance

*So, Father me yes Father me, I'll no longer be ashamed, to let
the tears flow down my face to be a child again,
I'll walk once more within your love, certain and assured, I'll
free the child that's here in me, and live my life restored.*

Life in the balance

Chapter Ten – A Fathers Faith

My dad died on July 7th 2002. This was a difficult time for us as a family. Until conversion, I hadn't always got on well with my dad, we, like many others had our ups and downs. We had our disagreements, quarrels and fights, but one thing I can honestly say is that I always knew that I had a dad who believed in me.

One of the most blessed things that has happened since becoming Christians, was that my dad and I were not only able to embrace one another as a father and son should be able to, but I was also able to kiss my dad, as well as tell him regularly that I loved him.

I so miss the daily visits I would make to dad, sitting with him, knowing he was in terrible pain, emotionally, and physically through the loss of mum, especially as he was also recovering from his own treatment.

Sitting in a restaurant with him one day, listening to him as he sought to encourage me, I recall thinking, "I will really miss this." Having a father who, no matter what, believes in you is an incredible encouragement.

It is so vital that we understand that our God is a God of the way through, it is also important we believe that He actually believes in us. The ultimate demonstration of that of course is the cross of Jesus. As a poster once said, "I asked the Lord how much do you love me?" He replied, "This much, spread open His arms and died."

Life in the balance

A friend of mine once told me of something they were told during one of their counselling sessions. They were told, "Do you realise that God trusts you with this problem?" It never really occurred to me before how much faith God often places in us, in the sense that He counts us so precious. He knows that the paths we traverse are not easy, but He has great faith in that which He has deposited within us, and He looks forward to the birthing that will indeed take place in our lives.

Our Father is 'faithful' He has faith in Himself, there is no higher source as it were, than God Himself.

Many years ago, after I had just left the Royal Navy I went through a difficult time settling back into civilian life. I had never known employment before I joined the Navy, the only previous job I had was a paper round. So, at 15 (and a half), I soon settled into the 'institutionalised' life the service offered. I never had to worry about anything, food, a roof over one's head, these were things I could take for granted.

I remember talking with my dad and explaining how difficult I was finding things. My first job on leaving the RN was as a milkman. That job lasted a matter of months due to the fact that I could not get my own round. I then did a stint at being an RAC sales patrolman, followed by a job selling books and magazines, (actually soft porn'). I then became a shop manager, and after I was sacked from that job I sold bean sprouts and mushrooms for a Chinese firm, also holding down a part time job in a pub, (which was not good for me considering my drinking habit). Finally, I ended up working in a news warehouse.

I felt to an extent lost, with no direction. Dad simply said to me, "don't worry son, you will find your way, I know you will." He believed in me, that is how I interpreted his words.

Life in the balance

You know, I can never think of a time where I have felt my dad was ever either disappointed in me, or perhaps ashamed of me. I was his son no matter what; at least that is what he always communicated to me. There have been times that I have needed to communicate that to my children. As we all know Pastor's kids are meant to be perfect. Well, Pastor's need to always make sure their kids know they are loved, even if they leave the church or grow disillusioned, or backslide.

I experienced so many problems when leaving the service. I had grown accustomed to the rewards of service life, work hard, keep your nose clean, and you will be rewarded. I thought I would experience the same philosophy in civilian life.

Whilst working as a manager of two shops, I had a very bad experience and entered a major dispute with my employers. I had been working from 5.00am until 7.00pm, six days a week. I also worked part of the day on Sunday. I was very unhappy and had started making a nuisance of myself. This resulted in me getting the sack, losing our home, (tied accommodation), and ending up in a real crisis.

Dad stood with us, and did all he could to help. No matter what my employers accused me of during my disciplinary hearing, dad would only believe the best of me.

As a pastor, I could never hide anything from my dad; he always seemed to know when I was struggling. In fact, he left us his journal that he kept; some of the personal things he has written in it concerning his kids reveal his belief in them.

This book is all about finding our way, and we need to know that we have a Father who believes in us. Even when we no longer believe in ourselves. Oh, I know we put our trust in Jesus, our faith is in His ability not our own. But there are

Life in the balance

times, especially when we face things like burn out, or failure that we lose our confidence, even our Godly confidence.

Remember Peter? Before he experienced failure through his denial he was told by Jesus quite clearly really of his future.

"Simon, Simon, Satan has asked to sift you as wheat. But I have prayed for you, Simon, that your faith may not fail. And when you have turned back, strengthen your brothers." Luke 22:31-32

The simple truth for us here is that God does not make mistakes, He makes heroes. It has been said that heroes are not born; they are forged in the fires of testing and refining.

Being sifted, facing failure and denial as Simon Peter did, experiencing the darkness and agony of facing up to your name, your character (even lack of it at times), your perceived moments of truth, your sins, your inadequacies and the like, are times when we could mistakenly believe that God had at last finished with us.

In those times we need to remind ourselves of our Fathers faith. When we use that expression, we are speaking of a Father who is faithful. He does not use us and simply discard us; it is very difficult in fact to remove you from His hand.

I heard of a preacher who had made an altar call, one of those who had responded was extremely upset, weeping, sobbing uncontrollably. The preacher asked him what it was he wanted from God. His response was to tell the preacher he had committed the unpardonable sin. The preacher's statement shocked the responder when he simply said, "No you have not." This seemed to anger the responder somewhat and he said, "But you do not understand, you don't know what I have done!" "That is true," said the preacher, "But I do know you are too sorry, for it to be unpardonable."

Life in the balance

I am sad to say that on more than one occasion I have come across Christians who make pronouncements over others. One day they love them; the next day they curse them, why? Because suddenly their perceptions of them change, due to the fact that they have become privy to information they didn't have previously.

Someone I love very much went through a terrible time during his walk with the Lord. He sinned. His sin was of a sexual nature, and the consequences were painful to say the least.

People, who had previously lauded him, now withdrew from him. Those who had made prophetic statements concerning his future ministry, and how God wanted to use him, changed them. In fact, he was told, God may still use you, but the anointing that was upon you will never be the same. In effect he was consigned to an existence where he would always feel that whatever he now had would only ever be second best. I was incensed. As if the consequences of an already seared conscience were not enough, guilt, shame and all of the accompanying problems involved in moving through repentance and into restoration. Some did not deem this enough; they still wanted to see further punishment.

This is someone who did not try and hide his sin, he confessed it, repented from it, faced up to the issues in his life that had been a seed bed, of the stumbling blocks for him. He went through 10 years or more trying to recapture a love from his Father he had never lost.

He spent agonising years trying to believe his Father would still use him. The irony was that he led more folks to Jesus as this apparent reject, failure, sinner, the man who once had an anointing or gifting, than any of those who changed their views over him.

Life in the balance

It would seem that God's view of him had not changed in any way. He was still loved, still accepted, still able to serve the Lord on exactly the same basis that he has always served him. It is as though some of us actually believe we are worthy in some way to be able to serve, that somehow, we have accumulated enough good points to be in the ministries we are in.

When I think of King David, his sin, yet clearly, there was still a heart after God. Sure enough, there were tragic consequences to his sin, as there are at times when we sin, do we really think that we should make those consequences even worse? Are we not told in scripture to restore one another 'gently?'

"Brothers, if someone is caught in a sin, you who are spiritual should restore him gently. But watch yourself, or you also may be tempted." Gal 6:1

No wonder we need 'fathers' in our churches. Those who know how to get alongside, they know how to lift back up again, they speak the healing words, they know how to deal with those who are caught in sin, without stripping them completely of any dignity whatsoever.

Surely enough damage has been done without further compounding the problem with our condemnation? If ever a person needs 'covering over' it is when they realise and confess their sin. Is that not what love does? Cover over?

I wrote a poem that I hope will encourage anyone else who may be tempted to think Father no longer believes in them...

"On that first day so long ago, you felt my love, my spirits flow,
You couldn't help but feel the pain, you brought your guilt, I cleansed the stain,
Do you remember child the words I said, they thrilled your heart, for you were now led,

Life in the balance

By greater joys, by deeper thrills, well, I remind you still……..I believe in you.

As you walked you sought my will, at times it seemed a bitter pill,
But true you stayed the course I set, and always at the cross we met,
And in that place of quiet and rest, I'd show you how you passed the test,
But now what's this I hear you say, you're insecure, you've lost your way,
Well I still remind you today………I believe in you.

Don't ere' forget your fathers heart, it can't be measured or pulled apart,
No matter what you do or say, I'll never leave or pull away,
You think that it's all up to you, but can't you see what's really true is…..I believe in you.

Oh yes! I know your secret ways, sins you've treasured – that lead astray,
And oh the pain as you realize, it's all a waste, built on lies,

Yet through it all I work my ways, they will lead you home to me again,
And you will learn about my love, and wonder, when still, like a dove,
I remain in you……..

Father's have an amazing ability to see the best in their kids. Our God has made a costly investment into our lives, and He expects to see fruit, despite the weeds that have also been planted. Despite our rebelliousness at times, or our sheer insensitivity and failure to seek His will.

I decided a few years ago that I would adopt another young man in our Church. Although both of his parents were still alive, neither, it would seem, wanted, or perhaps were able, to take responsibility for him any longer.

Life in the balance

Although in his twenties, emotionally he was still locked up, and desperately needed someone to love him as only a father can. He was on drugs, and was used by some as a 'fixer,' that is, he would be called upon to go around and sort someone out. I knew deep down inside he was hurting, and needed someone to believe in him. It was to be a long job, four years in fact before seeing real fruit. I would turn up at his work place, he would push me away, testing me, trying to discover how long it would be before I too would write him off.

He did all kinds of crazy things, even pulling a gun on someone and ending up in cells, after an armed police response unit was sent to look for him, and my son who was driving the car they were in. Someone had to take responsibility for him, so I talked with the Chief Inspector, who decided to let him off with a warning, after a while in cells, to cool his heels as it were.

Many would have considered him to be finished as a Christian. He had grown up through our youth program, starting in the Sunday school, even joining in with the football team now and then. But as far as many were concerned because he didn't attend the church he was not interested.

I believed differently. I am now pleased to say that as my 'spiritually adopted' son, he is currently attending the Elim School of Ministry, having started his own ministry, reaching out to street kids in the area. There is a huge difference between being a teacher, and being a father. Fathers show that they believe in you. Fathers do not back off, just because some less flattering aspects of a persons character come to the fore, that is the time fathers move in closer. I would add at this point that I 'publicly' made it known I had spiritually adopted this young man, and I did not wait until he was 'sorted out' as it were. I did it during what could be seen as his worst times.

Life in the balance

Why? Because that is when he needed someone to believe in him the most.

Oh! it was fun! Phone calls like, "can you come and see me, I've just been sacked from my job, I gave someone a slap. He asked for it."

The Crabb family in early 2000.
Front row left to right, Catherine (daughter), Sheila, myself, Madison (Granddaughter), Mary Jane (daughter in law), Peter (son), back row left to right, Mark (son in law), Danny (adopted son). I hope you would agree with me, that I have the look of a blessed man in this photograph. Since then we have a further six grandchildren.

My own personal conviction is that there are some really good kids around. They may not measure up in the 'religious sense,' that is, they do not always meet our 'doctrinal' criteria. We

Life in the balance

have discovered that raising our children has meant loving them no matter what.

Fathers to a degree, take responsibility for their kids. I was given the opportunity to adopt once again when meeting my son's future wife Mary Jane. She has a daughter Madison, so in one go I have adopted another daughter and also a granddaughter.

She has come from a background where she has not known the security of being 'fathered,' without it costing her something, and to have someone who is now encouraging her, believing in her is a totally new experience. She has not experienced what it is like to be part of a family where unconditional love is the foundation. To be able to pass on that which I am receiving in terms of my relationships with my heavenly Father, and that which I learnt through my earthly father is a tremendous privilege.

I am also discovering the difference between being a leader and being a father. Fathers love to see their children do well, to even exceed their own accomplishments. They will do all that is necessary for that to take place. Even when it involves recognising that often they do it better than you. I am blessed with an assistant Pastor who is able to do many things better than myself. It is a blessing, not a threat. This applies to my eldership as well. I love to see them excel, to realise their dreams, to step aside when need be.

Life in the balance

Our Garden (a song of thanksgiving for my wife)

In the garden of my life, I felt so alone,
I had so much I could share, that had always been my own,
But as I felt that empty space, I looked and there I saw a face,
And then I knew that it was time, to share with you all that was mine.

For it is God's own mystery,
How you can be so close to me,
And now two lives become entwined,
For I am yours and you are mine.

In a garden there are tree's of many kinds,
And each one bears a fruit that has a taste divine,
And now our lives become a glade,
Of different tree's of many shades,
And we'll both eat from the one vine,
Until the fullness of our time.

For it is God's own mystery,
How you can be so close to me,
And now two lives become entwined,
For I am yours and you are mine.

And through the seasons of our years, our gardens changed and grown,
There's been much pain, and many tears, but we are not alone,
For there is one who prunes and cares, for all the things we love and share,
He grows the fruit to make the wine, from love that's stood the test of time.

For it is Gods own mystery………………

Life in the balance

Chapter eleven – Weighing up

"Lord, forgive these hasty words, which flowed from this tongue of mine,
And though I'd say it was done through hurt, I know it's more to do with pride,
Yes, I find it hard to tell you, of things I've hidden for so long,
I know that they're the things that hurt you, yes they are,
And if I'd realised I'd have seen how very wrong,
A child can be, when he's not listening,
If I could have seen what I was missing,
If I'd known through all my trying,
Just how my soul was crying,
And when I felt like I was dying,
You broke through to me, and you set me free.

Oh Lord how could I say to you, I am hidden from your eyes,
I know it's just not true, but I persist with all these lies,
Yet when it seems so dark around me, and I am filled with bitterness,
I fight you like a man who's drowning,
Until I'm weary and I need a place to rest,
And then I hear what you are saying,
And I find the paths you're making,
Then I see how much you love me,
For I feel your heart within me,
It is time for reality, and I am free, yes I am free.

Oh, Father I know I've found that place, where I can praise you from my heart,
And though I know I've wasted time, I want to make a brand-new start,

Life in the balance

I've emptied all I had within me, that you might fill me once again,
No more the fruitless days of trying, for it's your spirit who fills my mouth with praise,
And I will sing of all your goodness, and I will tell of all your faithfulness,
I will lift my hands to touch you, I will give my heart to love you,
I will come into your throne room, for I am free yes I am free,
And I have made a brand new start.

There comes a time, believe me, no matter how hard the road has been, that you begin to 'weigh up' where you have actually been, and as a result begin to see the road ahead with a little more clarity.

It is a humbling process that we have been looking at. And I refer once again to something I mentioned earlier, "are we really willing for God to answer our prayers?" When I recall some of my prayers I am at the least embarrassed when I realise that I made them with an attitude that verged on believing, perhaps God was reluctant to hear.

That somehow through 'my faith' 'my persistence' I will succeed in getting a reluctant God to hear me. My pride in fact, was the hindrance in seeing my prayers answered, it was as though I saw everything else or even everyone else as the problem, when in fact God needed me to see the 'need in me' first. In fact, I believe there is no real substitute for people coming to father for themselves, for it is then that sometimes father reveals something to us, which may eventually have relevance for others.

It is one thing being able to preach principles, or even methodology to others, stirring messages that are truth to the

Life in the balance

minds of those listening, yet at times lack real incarnational value.

We can be 'theologically correct' in something, but truth we probably realise is to an extent robbed of some value until it is really tested in us. Knowledge is somewhat lessened in value until it is applied, and the application can often be during the most difficult and trying of circumstances.

There are some principles in scripture that at times in my life I have found relatively easy to apply. But then it seems as though hedges of protection around me are removed for some reason, and the truth is challenged in me. It is then I truly need faith in Gods word and discover the need to 'stand firm.'

Oft' times I have succeeded in doing this, yet if truth be said there are my moments of failure, yet in it all during the 'weighing up' process one discovers that our failure is a mere stepping stone in discovering His opportunities to grow. To grow means to change, and to change involves humility.

As I have discovered, there is an alternative to humbling ourselves, and that is, for God to humble us. This in fact, is a demonstration of His love for us, for if we are trapped in a place where we really do not see our great need for Him, we are in that dreaded place where we are neither hot nor cold. Alternatively, we can in arrogance, almost presuppose that there is little in us that needs to change, or even that we have reached a place of satisfaction with ourselves.

The 'weighing up' time in our lives is often a time of re-learning. We can often see all kinds of things. Times of discipline. Times of Gods grace, and protection.

For me personally, as I look back over some of the moments when I was almost in despair, I am able to thank God that He did not allow me doorways of escape that I am sure I may well

Life in the balance

have jumped through. He knew what was best for me, and at what time. Though at times his hand seemed heavy upon me, and I thought and said hasty things in my petulance concerning his faithfulness, nevertheless He showed Himself to be totally trustworthy.

I am beginning to see just what it must have been like for God to even withhold his hand, during times that His children cry out to Him to intervene. What goes through our Father's heart as He watches with anticipation as one of his precious ones arrives at a crossroads and seeks, and weighs up, the way through.

I have discovered that it takes humility to pray, and it takes even more humility to receive the answers to those prayers, particularly if they were truly spirit lead. The Holy Spirit will always cause us to seek the Fathers will, which nearly always involves us changing, us becoming less, Him becoming greater. Change is here to stay.

As I am 'weighing up' I can see how sometimes I have actually been the hindrance to my prayers being answered. Arrogance, judgmentalism, insecurities, refusing to face the truth in my own life.

When I read of revival I discover that they all involve people changing in incredible ways. The changes in their lives came as a result of revival. There was of course some change in the hearts of people evidenced by an increased sense of need, a desire for change, a humbling of self, a repentant attitude, but the changes that take place in the communities affected by revival are as a result of the increased measure of the Lords presence amongst his people. But it all began with humility in someone's heart, seeing their own desperate need for God to change them.

Life in the balance

The amazing thing about some of the people that God seems to be able to use so easily is that when you study them you discover that many of them had incomplete, even insufficient theologies. But because of their humility and sincerity of heart God was able to use them mightily for His purposes.

'Weighing up' for me is keeping me in a position of humility for it involves constant re-education in the things of God. It also causes me to want to remain humble in His sight. It is not a matter of self-condemnation or anything like it, in fact quite the opposite. Knowing the truth actually brings incredible release into one's life for it also involves the stripping away of falsity, and the freedom from the power of expectation either from yourself or others.

Fear, the great enemy of faith, in that similarly it has creative power, is also dealt a major blow as we 'weigh up.' For weighing up begins to acknowledge the wonderful ways of God. His ways of course are higher than ours; His thoughts are higher than ours. But as we look at where we have been, the paths we have traversed, the mountains that have been removed, the roads of hindrance we may well have travelled had we refused to submit to the God of the way through, we are filled with awe.

Our faith is increased based purely upon the evidence of that which is unseen. However, the evidence of the changed life is there for all to see. So, 'weighing up' becomes an incredible faith building experience.

As with that lovely poem, 'Footprints' we can see the footprints of our God clearly with us through all the roads we had believed were so lonely, desperate, dry and at times despairing. He was there, always, constant and faithful, leading us forward. The only times He was not there was if we turned aside on what appeared to be an easier path.

Life in the balance

Perhaps you are one of those who feel as though they have been upon a circuitous road of rebellion, involving you sinning in ways you never thought possible, settling for a time with a life of compromise and mediocrity.

If you are reading this book, it is likely it is because you are sick of that life, and are looking for a way back. Well, again I would say the way back has to be in the same direction as the way through.

It is likely that you began on this road of rebellion for a reason. Perhaps you were tempted off the narrow road, frightened off it, discouraged off, whatever the reason; you will probably find you are back at the point where you left. That could cause you to feel as though you are now miles behind where you should be, and is it worth all the effort to get back on the road?

Very simply, yes it is. If you truly get back on the road of obedience and holiness the lessons you will have learnt whilst away from the centre of Gods purpose for your life can be turned to your advantage. He is the great restorer, nothing is wasted, and He can turn what appears to be useless and desolate into something useful and fruitful.

Once you are again walking in His purpose for your life, you will be amazed as you look back at how quickly those wasted years seem to fall away behind you. You will discover, as I have and still am, that many of those who seem to be so greatly used by God, walk with a limp.

Some of them have thorns in their flesh, some can still tell you of great sorrows or disappointments, losses, times of incredible barrenness. But they will all tell you of a God who took them through, and helped them to discover the right road, the kings' highway.

Life in the balance

Chapter Twelve The Way Through

Isaiah 35 *"The desert and the parched land will be glad; the wilderness will rejoice and blossom. Like the crocus, it will burst into bloom; it will rejoice greatly and shout for joy.
The glory of Lebanon will be given to it, the splendor of Carmel and Sharon; they will see the glory of the LORD,
the splendor of our God. Strengthen the feeble hands,
steady the knees that give way; say to those with fearful hearts, "Be strong, do not fear; your God will come, he will come with vengeance; with divine retribution he will come to save you." Then will the eyes of the blind be opened
and the ears of the deaf unstopped. Then will the lame leap like a deer, and the mute tongue shout for joy. Water will gush forth in the wilderness and streams in the desert. The burning sand will become a pool, the thirsty ground bubbling springs.
In the haunts where jackals once lay, grass and reeds and papyrus will grow. And a highway will be there; it will be called the Way of Holiness. The unclean will not journey on it; it will be for those who walk in that Way; wicked fools will not go about on it. No lion will be there, nor will any ferocious beast get up on it; they will not be found there. But only the redeemed will walk there, and the ransomed of the LORD will return. They will enter Zion with singing; everlasting joy will crown their heads. Gladness and joy will overtake them, and sorrow and sighing will flee away."*

In the early stages of my life, for whatever reasons, I learnt to run away. Running away, I was to discover was in fact no way, for the things I ran away from would keep appearing in different forms throughout my life. There was always something to run away from.

Life in the balance

Fear will keep you 'frozen' until the day you realise you are 'chosen' to walk the paths that God prepares for you. Without doubt those paths will have obstacles on them very carefully designed and disguised, but are opportunities for you to grow.

Pressures of all kinds will come upon us, and even develop within us. And as we learn to press on through the pressure we enter times in our lives where we must face up to the past in order to change the way in which we deal with things.

At times things get very stormy in our lives; however, we see it through, realising, even during the agony of a long dry desert, that there are no short cuts. In those times God provides quiet waters where we can be refreshed and renewed in order that we can press on still further.

If we remain Spirit led we will avoid drinking from the polluted holes, until we come to a time when all that has been going on within us is ready to be birthed, as it were, in our lives.

That birthing process we learn is going to require some effort on our part, and perhaps even a loss of dignity, a time for travailing not wailing.

Through it all we will see that we have a Father who has faith in that which He has deposited within us, if we truly cooperate with Him we will without doubt make it through with Him. Then, as we 'weigh up' and look back upon the road we have been travelling on we are enlightened to the ways of our God.

And so we come to this time of the 'way through.' In my own experience what I am beginning to see is that this way through was not necessarily a mere directional issue. It was not a mere issue of moving in the right or wrong direction; it was more to do with the means of my moving.

Life in the balance

In other words, I often had the right end in view, but the motivations, power, the means was what was now in question. You see, it is not only the end that is important, the 'means to the end' is equally vital.

We are here to glorify God, not ourselves. Therefore, the methods that we use are so very important, for they will either glorify God, or they will bring Gods name into disrepute.

"This is the message we have heard from him and declare to you: God is light; in him there is no darkness at all. If we claim to have fellowship with him yet walk in the darkness, we lie and do not live by the truth. But if we walk in the light, as he is in the light, we have fellowship with one another, and the blood of Jesus, his Son, purifies us from all sin.
If we claim to be without sin, we deceive ourselves and the truth is not in us. If we confess our sins, he is faithful and just and will forgive us our sins and purify us from all unrighteousness. If we claim we have not sinned, we make him out to be a liar and his word has no place in our lives." 1 John1:5-10

We can see now I hope that some times to get the means right means facing up to some of the less flattering parts of our characters and call upon the Lord to help us to change.

We have seen how pressure can magnify these things, and how God does not judge us for what we are, but for refusing to become what we are meant to be. So, often He will bring us to 'crisis' in order that with Him, we can see what is actually there.

Gods view of course is not limited to time and space, as ours is. He can see us from the perspective of eternity, He can see us in our completion, as we are meant to be. In this we

Life in the balance

understand that we are a work that is constantly in progress, and as long as we continue to progress, God is pleased.

This facing up process that we have looked at needs to be brought to a completion. That is, I do not believe we should remain in an attitude of analysis that keeps us stationary or inert.

We need to ensure that any gaps in the circle of our lives are closed, so in a sense this would be seen as the final step in the process of having faced up to weaknesses, insecurities, sin, and the like.

With regard to sin for instance, the teaching in scripture is clear. Sin creates a gap, and is a potential foot hold to the enemy from which he will continue to seek to harass us. If it is an area of sin that we have had to face up to then the circle must be closed through confession and repentance from that sin – we are still talking about change.

If it is a deficiency in our character, an insecurity, an unchallenged thought process (stronghold) then again there needs to be a closing if we are to move on, in order to grow in other areas.

The enemy, we know, is prowling around like a roaring lion, in order to seek to take advantage of any perceived areas where the circle of our life is still open.

Resentments can so easily turn into deep-seated bitterness, even hatred. Disobedience could develop into a stronghold where the enemy has a level of control through that particular person, even bringing disruption into the body of Christ.

We need to see our lives from the correct perspective. Someone once put it this way, "I am not a mere human being

Life in the balance

having a temporary spiritual experience, I am a spiritual being having a temporary human experience."

We will encounter constant harassment from evil forces, the last thing the enemy wants is believers committed to a path or purpose that is constantly closing doors, as they progress, behind them, leaving no potential entry points whatsoever.

He desires to attempt to break in through any potential areas. That means believers, refusing to allow him any footholds. If it were not possible for him to gain a foothold the bible would not warn against it. Habits are areas we need to be very careful in.

On a personal level I am very wary over anything in my life I feel the need to defend. Something can be permissible, but is it beneficial? Not only to me, but perhaps to others also. Is what I am doing or being an offence or hindrance or stumbling block to anyone else in fellowship with me?

Someone once asked me, "How can I stop the enemy, how can I make him leave me alone?" My initial reaction to that question is to say; you will never get the enemy to stop doing what he is purposed to do, that is, he is a liar, he hates Christians, and he will prowl around like a roaring lion.

I guess one way would be to bore him to death. Do not offer him anything. He can only take what you offer him. Jesus said regarding the prince of this world, "He has nothing in me." No point of contact with the enemy, this is achieved through submitting to God, then we are in the position to resist the enemy, and we are told he will flee.

So, we must take responsibility for our lives in the sense that we seek to ensure there are no breaks in the circle of our lives.

Life in the balance

Being in the light with one another is a good way of achieving this. As we humble ourselves one to another, confessing our sins, our faults, our weaknesses, having others pray for us, all good ways of shoring up potential areas of interference.

"When an evil spirit comes out of a man, it goes through arid places seeking rest and does not find it. Then it says, 'I will return to the house I left.' When it arrives, it finds the house unoccupied, swept clean and put in order. Then it goes and takes with it seven other spirits more wicked than itself, and they go in and live there. And the final condition of that man is worse than the first. That is how it will be with this wicked generation." Mt 12:43-45

We can enter a season in our lives when our house as it were, is swept clean. We perhaps either confess a sin, or face up to a persistent insecurity, but we fail to repent. That is, we do not change. We continue to walk in a fleshly kind of way that does not involve trusting the Lord, and so we fail to close the circle. We do not find the way through. In effect we are still on the run. We will constantly be hit by the enemy in the areas that he believes he stands a chance of gaining a foothold in.

I have seen this kind of thing happen, when a person gets into a sin, confess habit, but sees little or no change in an area of their lives. The circle must be closed, the issue must be resolved, the distractions and hindrances avoided, the way through sought, and the matter finally dealt with. This will only be done from a place of humility and dependence upon God.

I was listening to a ministry tape recently by 'Joseph Garlington' who was spoken to, through watching an Indiana Jones movie. It is the one where they are seeking the Holy Grail. His father, played by Sean Connery, has joined him, and

Life in the balance

they come to the place where some nefarious character has them cornered.

They arrive at the entrance to a tunnel, which apparently leads to the cave where they will find the grail. There are three clues as to how they will be able to get past the tests that await those who seek the Holy Grail. They are: -

1. Only the penitent man shall pass
2. You must walk on the name of God
3. You must leap from the Lions mouth

They have already sent one man through who instantly dies, understandably no one else is particularly keen to follow suit. Indiana is told he must go, obviously he refuses and so his father is shot. In horror Indiana is then told, "Mr Jones you need to decide what you really believe."

Now his belief is that the Holy Grail will bring healing to his father and so he has no choice but to attempt to pass through.

The answer to the first clue suddenly comes to him and he drops to his knees, just in time to avoid some whirring blades that would have taken off his head.

"Submit yourselves, then, to God. Resist the devil, and he will flee from you. Come near to God and he will come near to you. Wash your hands, you sinners, and purify your hearts, you double-minded. Grieve, mourn and wail. Change your laughter to mourning and your joy to gloom. Humble yourselves before the Lord, and he will lift you up. James 4:7-10

Remember how Joshua is on his knees when he sees a creature with a drawn sword. Joshua approaches him and says, *"Are*

Life in the balance

you for us or for our enemies," the response is, *"as commander of the Lords hosts I have come."*

I have spoken about humility already but that is the first place we will come to in order to find the way through with our God.

"This is the one I esteem: he who is humble and contrite in spirit, and trembles at my word". Isaiah 66:2

In humility we realize that everything we do must be done in His strength not our own. In Jesus name, not our own names or for our own glory.

We do not need to be full of ourselves; we need to be full of Him. And of course, the leap from the Lions mouth can be seen as the walk we walk being one of absolute faith in Him and His abilities. Having absolute faith in His character.
I wonder, is it possible that you have been pressing forward in the things of God, and suddenly for some reason you find yourself in a howling waste?

I met someone a long time ago that actually believed God was going to kill him. He was sinning, in fact he was addicted to pornography, disgusted with himself, yet still helplessly clinging to the very thing that was destroying him.

His misbelief was that he had to get the victory, not accepting that Jesus had done that already. His belief was that once he had overcome this addiction that he would be loved and accepted by God, not believing that, *"But God demonstrates his own love for us in this: While we were still sinners, Christ died for us."* Romans 5:8

He had forgotten that God is the God of the way through, He is absolutely faithful, do not be so discouraged that you are

Life in the balance

tempted to think that perhaps He has just left you all alone, to walk a walk so dark, so despairing and so difficult that God has distanced Himself to the extent that you are ready to simply give in.

"Those whom I love I rebuke and discipline. So be earnest, and repent. Here I am! I stand at the door and knock. If anyone hears my voice and opens the door, I will come in and eat with him, and he with me. To him who overcomes, I will give the right to sit with me on my throne, just as I overcame and sat down with my Father on his throne. He who has an ear, let him hear what the Spirit says to the churches." Rev 3:19-22

There is a path planned out for you to walk, His plan for you is to walk it, never on your own, with Him leading you. We often quote the passage from Jeremiah 29:11 that declares, *"I know the plans I have for you."* There is your source then if you want to know what they are. "plans to give you hope, and a future."

Take heart, keep to His paths, if there are things in your life to face up to, do so, humble yourself, do not allow your past to determine your future.

"Not that I have already obtained all this, or have already been made perfect, but I press on to take hold of that for which Christ Jesus took hold of me. Brothers, I do not consider myself yet to have taken hold of it. But one thing I do: Forgetting what is behind and straining toward what is ahead, I press on toward the goal to win the prize for which God has called me heavenward in Christ Jesus." Philippians 3:12-14

Yes, I know that you know these scriptures, but are they incarnating within you? I urge you if you are facing things, not

Life in the balance

to play with them, remember a bad root is not for observing or analyzing in some way, it is for plucking out.

As I have faced up to things in my own life I am able to say that as I continue on the path of the way through, with the God of the way through, that I have every confidence He will bring me through. And although there are moments that I experience many if not all of the things outlined in this book, there are also the moments of incredible acceleration.

Life in the balance

Chapter Thirteen He has nothing in me

John 14:30
2 Corinthians 10:3-5

Jesus was crucified, at Golgotha, "The place of the skull." And it is precisely there that all warfare is initiated – in the mind. It is one thing identifying problems, issues, sins, past hurts and the like, and as I have stressed it is no good to do these things with the intention of merely analysing, sympathising and even comparing with others.

If we identify a diseased root, then it must be plucked out. If we confess a sin, it must be repented from completely, not toyed with.

In fact, I have discovered in my own pilgrimage that anything in our lives that could potentially defend the enemy must be removed. This is what real deliverance is all about. If we are experiencing constant harassment from the enemy in an area, it is likely that the reason is because there is still a potential stronghold for him to play around in.

I believe that when the apostle speaks of pulling down strongholds, he is talking about the demolition and removal of old ways of thinking, in order that the presence of Jesus can be more fully made manifest from within us.

Really, a stronghold in effect defines a fortress where an enemy can hide and gain some degree of protection. These strongholds exist in the thought patterns and ideas that govern either Individuals, churches, communities, and perhaps even nations.

Life in the balance

Before anyone sins in a physical sense, it is almost certain that they will have experienced what I would call sympathetic thought processes towards wickedness.

Arguments, pretensions, against the knowledge of God. What I am learning still is that the Lord is seeking to get me to face any potential areas where the enemy could conceivably seek to use as a source of defence, or indeed an argument against the knowledge of God.

So, when our Lord Jesus said, *"He has nothing in me,"* He means that there was nothing in himself that the enemy could use as a means of defence. There were no thought processes in Jesus that Satan could use to try and develop into a stronghold.

I want to say right now, understanding that this may well upset some people's interpretation of scripture, that I do not believe a born-again spirit filled Christian can be possessed by the enemy. I do believe, however, that a believer can give place to the enemy, a foothold, even for a strong hold to be developed that will cause them to be at times even violently oppressed in their thoughts.

Thoughts, which can sympathise with the old self-life, that are contrary to God and His word.

In the past I have prayed with all kinds of people. Folks have responded during a time of ministry and want deliverance from this or that. Whenever the power encounter takes place, it is vital that there is also a truth encounter. Jesus said, "Then you will know the truth, and the truth will set you free."

For the truth to set us free, we must know it. That goes beyond a mere intellectual understanding. Truth will be tested in us, in order that we can truly appropriate it for ourselves, and learn to minister it into the lives of those around us.

Life in the balance

I am sure you have all heard the amusing story of the little boy who insists on standing up on the back seat of his father's car. His father turns around, and tells the boy to sit down, after a short time of disobedience, reluctantly he sits down. However, he is heard to mutter, *"I might be sitting down, but I am standing up on the inside."*

That is what some Christians do. On the outside they are doing the right thing, but on the inside sometimes, something else is going on. If that is the case, then there are potential areas of sympathy either with the flesh or even with the enemy. You cannot merely cast out this disobedience. However, the sympathetic thought processes that allow a stronghold to develop certainly need to be brought down. We are told that the double minded man is unstable in all he does. I recall hearing Jim McConnell from Whitewell once say, *"A man with no heart is to be pitied, a man with two hearts is a monster."*

For example. When speaking with those who have fallen into a serious sexual sin, I almost always discover that there was an extended time, where sympathetic thought processes were either entertained, or even, fantasised over.

People rarely suddenly decide to backslide. Things can occur that act like triggers that to an extent, if played with, can cause the self-life to be stimulated to respond.

I ministered to someone who was going about some DIY work in a bedroom, (some details changed) and happened to glance across the road from the window, and noticed a young woman undressing. Something within him was captivated. Instead of immediately dealing with this he dallied a while, watching with increasing interest. Actually, when ministering to a men's group fairly recently I asked what they would have done in a

Life in the balance

situation like this. One honest soul shouted out, *"I would have probably fetched a telescope."*

Well before he knew it, within moments he was indeed captivated, he watched and watched, returning at times in the hope that he would witness something like this again.

Although he did not have that opportunity again, he was now fantasising with it, carefully protecting that part of himself, not exposing it or dealing with it at all, it was not long before he found other ways of fulfilling the increased need within him.

He started to view pornography, even purchasing magazines, but usually looking for sites on the internet. At this point one of two things will occur. Either some kind of crisis will occur forcing you to face up to this mountain, or things will continue until another moral line is crossed. Some seem to think that the fact they are not 'caught out' or challenged is an indication that God is willing to put up with it. It does not occur to them that sometimes it is actually the enemy who gives a level of protection.

When it becomes a public sin, that is, perhaps an affair, or even in some cases a person visiting a prostitute In order to fulfil some kind of unresolved fantasy, all kinds of damage is caused.

This is why we are exhorted in scripture to make our thoughts obedient to Christ Jesus. Satan and his co-horts feed on sin, and where there is a sin habit in the life of a believer you can guarantee there will be satanic activity. Bringing the believer into condemnation, oppression, a lack of joy or peace, until eventually they are crushed in some way.

This is why my friends we need to know the God of the 'way through.' As we are determined to press on, despite whatever

Life in the balance

pressure we are under or in, as we are humbly willing to face up to the areas in our lives where there are either damaged or weak bricks as it were. Then we will continue ever onwards, growing, learning and seeing measurable progress in our lives.

We are exhorted in 1 Peter 1:13-16 *"Therefore, prepare your minds for action; be self-controlled; set your hope fully on the grace to be given you when Jesus Christ is revealed. As obedient children, do not conform to the evil desires you had when you lived in ignorance. But just as he who called you is holy, so be holy in all you do; for it is written: "Be holy, because I am holy."*

I recall on one occasion when speaking along these lines someone saying to me, *"The Jesus you are preaching is becoming too intense, too confrontational, we need more grace,"* but, grace always comes with truth.

I made mention earlier of the time Joshua was confronted by the 'commander of the Lords host.' I have learnt that when I want greater victories, I can expect a greater revelation of the Lord.

Imagine getting a revelation like this one! A holy warrior dressed for war, with his sword drawn. I cannot remember where I heard this now, but I heard or read this, "Imagine for a moment the Lord Jesus Christ stood before you with a drawn sword, the tip of that sword is aimed right at your heart."

You see, we have this idea that Jesus is on our side, actually as Joshua discovered afresh, we are on His side. If we are going to truly wield the sword of the spirit, that sword must first of all pass through our own hearts.

As I seek to follow the God of the way through, He is showing me that in order to be able to confront the strongholds in the

Life in the balance

lives of others, He will come to my house and do some re-arranging first.

You see, the character and nature of the good shepherd, gentle Jesus, are no less true, simply because another aspect of His character is revealed to us.

I began this book by saying that I have discovered that I love a Father who is totally uncompromising. When He reveals things within me that are to be challenged, I know and understand, and now accept, that we are going to find the way through. If I keep hold of Him it will always result in victory.

Many times, I have been left with reminders, especially when the valley has been long and hard. But I have always found that because He loves me so much, He will not let me off the hook, though I fight Him tooth and nail, though I manipulate, even when I try to run, He is able to show me just how insistent He can be.

"So, I say to you, give up the fight,
For it's not by power, or by might,
But by my Spirit you will be,
The son creation waits to see,
For you're the picture I will paint,
A masterpiece without a taint,
For every good work takes its time,
But I'll finish it for you are mine."
(portrait song)

Remember child of God; time is what the Lord says it is. No matter how long the road seems, no matter how hard, His intention is that you will reach the end of it, whenever that is.
He has a place He is taking us to, and He will get us there, but Watch out! There are enemies on the way through! The

Life in the balance

destination is worth it all, the way through is the only way to go……………………..

Life in the balance

Chapter Fourteen Anchors Away, All Ahead Full

I am sure you do not need me to explain what an anchor is, or what it is for. Their design has not changed all that much over the years, although there are many different sorts. Primitive anchors held a vessel only by their enormous weight and friction along the sea bottom.

However, the design of modern sea anchors enables them to dig into the underwater surface and grip the seabed, against the drift of the vessel. Larger ships will often carry several anchors, and they can be used even in slowing a ship down, as well as for mooring purposes.

Obviously, what we have been looking at in this book are some of the methods that God uses, to either slow us down, or indeed stop us altogether, and even hold us in a particular position until His purpose is fulfilled.

No doubt you are aware of the principle in the Old Testament, that when the children of Israel were on the move they kept a watch on the cloud above the tent of meeting. When the cloud moved, they moved. When the cloud stood still, so did they.

It is of distinct advantage that we develop a listening ear to the Lord in these matters. If we want to avoid those times when God has to stop us, because we are just not listening as well as we should be.

I remember one particular ship that I was on while in the Navy. It was a large vessel, and often we would have to anchor off somewhere, because the harbour was just not large enough.

Life in the balance

On one occasion, we were informed that the skipper was going to attempt entering harbour 'stern first,' that is, reversing in. It was a tricky manoeuvre, made all the more interesting, because the American Navy was observing with keen interest as Her Majesty's best came in.

HMS Fife, a County class Guided Missile Destroyer, built in 1963, now serving in the Chilean Navy as "Blanco Encalada." My first ship, I joined her in 1972 and served on her for two and a half years.

This was in fact the captain's last entrance into a foreign port, for he was then leaving the ship having been promoted to Commodore. He was obviously very keen to make a good impression, and to leave the ship having done what the port authorities said was not possible.

A young sub-lieutenant was on the quarterdeck, and his job was to call out how far we were from the harbour wall, so that the captain could accurately gauge the moment he should disengage power. Everything was going extremely well, the

Life in the balance

Americans seemed mightily impressed, the captain was buoyant – all was well, and therefore we were very confidant that in a very short space of time we would be enjoying a run ashore.

The sub lieutenant had, every few seconds been calling out – 300 yards sir, 200 yards sir, then suddenly – 3 feet sir, bang. An awful shudder went through the whole ship, the Americans cheered, the captain turned purple, we all turned away from him in order to hide the expressions on our faces, the Stornophone (similar to a walkie talkie) went extremely quiet, although all of this only took mere seconds, it seemed as though half a day had passed by.

The damage was quite extensive and meant that we had to remain in harbour longer than was originally anticipated (shame). The simple point being we would have been better off anchoring off, and had we done so, this unfortunate incident would not have occurred.

Sure, being at anchor could be inconvenient. It meant having to run liberty boats, it also meant not having the advantages of being alongside a nice long harbour wall, being able to run off shore power. Supplying the ship was far easier when in harbour, everything was so much slower when at anchor, and of course you were pretty much at the mercy of the weather. If the weather got really bad you simply had to move.

There were good points as well. For instance, if you were anchored in a particularly pleasant spot you could often go swimming. Also, coming back from a run ashore was an interesting experience. I recall a pal of mine attempting to smuggle a couple of bottles of vodka in a carrier bag. The officer of the watch challenged him, and said, "young man, I am going to turn my back, and I want to hear two distinct splashes."

Life in the balance

Sure enough, he turned his back, and there came the sound of two distinct splashes as apparently the bottles of vodka were disposed of. In fact, my pal had thrown his shoes over the side and was quickly in the process of descending down the main hatch. I'm not sure to this day whether the officer of the watch knew what had happened, it is entirely possible he let him off for his shear audacity. It was an interesting evening for some in the mess deck that night.

It is not necessarily a pleasant experience when it seems as though God has dropped anchor, and you are going nowhere. It is easy to begin to imagine all kinds of reasons for it. Of course, what we need to understand is that many times God is simply enabling us to avoid a disaster.

Sometimes He drops the anchors that are meant to merely slow us down, other times He stops us for a period of time. Some anchors can be used to help manoeuvre, or even turn a ship. When we are seeking to weigh up the way through it is wise that we learn to listen to the one who is leading us through. If He says drop anchor that is exactly what He means, and it is for a purpose.

That moment will come when you will hear those words you have been waiting for, *"All ahead full."* I have discovered that all that had held me fast, slowed me down, distracted me, or demanded my attention, has suddenly disappeared. Then there is this incredible time of forging forward at a speed that is sometimes totally exhilarating. No longer distracted with inner concerns, no more excuses, no more compromising, maybe even no more sinning in a particular area.

I will never forget the day that I was released from the Royal Navy. I had completed my leaving routine. A procedure where you visited various departments to get your leaving chitty

Life in the balance

stamped. Ensuring you had returned all your kit, your identity documents, and that you had received your resettlement interview. That was an experience that lasted about five minutes. I sat before a careers officer, he looked rather disdainfully at me and said, "If you don't join the police force you're a !*?!*? idiot." That was it, interview over, after that I decided to spend my one Months resettlement training with the RSPCA. I had always loved animals, though I thoroughly enjoyed the experience my main reason for choosing it was to be close to Sheila for that time.

On return, I stood in an office awaiting my leaving papers. As the Petty Officer handed them to me I realised that was it, once I left the base I was officially a civilian. I almost ran to my mini van, jumped in, and as I was going out of the gates of HMS Nelson I shouted something to the officer of the watch that did not really bless him, gesticulated to him in a very un-naval fashion, and certainly in a way that left him in no doubt as to whether or not I had just saluted him, gunned my little 850cc engine, and drove as fast as I could to Rugby. I was convinced that I was now free! Nothing would get in my way ever again, now, all that I had hoped for was before me. Little did I know what I was carrying 'within me,' or what lay 'ahead of me' in terms of facing up and growing. All that I had ran from still lay within me and would one day have to be faced up to.

That was in May 1979. In the year 2000, God took me back to visit a Royal Navy ship. For some strange reason I entered a competition in our local newspaper and the first prize was a visit on board HMS Tireless, a nuclear submarine. I just knew I was going to win, and that I would be taking that trip. I did. With the mayor of Rugby, and the commanding officer of the local sea cadet unit, I went to Plymouth and was given accommodation in the wardroom of HMS Drake.

Life in the balance

I had a wonderful time. A healing took place within me as I was able to appreciate some of the good things that had happened within me since leaving. What I didn't know about was revealed to me a few weeks later. A couple in our Church had been touched by my testimony, especially about my time in the Navy, they asked God specifically to send me back and heal me, and use me in some way. They never said anything, they simply prayed. Since then I was appointed as a sea cadet chaplain, and I sit on the HMS Tireless affiliation committee.

The memory that gives me the most amusement is this. As I stepped onto the gangway of the Submarine, several Naval personnel (including the captain) stood to attention and piped me on board. As I reached the brow of the boat they saluted me as a VIP would be. I couldn't believe it, and chuckled to myself as I was warmly greeted and welcomed on board. I had a strange thought as I suddenly thought back and remembered the young lad who was told to, *"Switch on his night vision."* Memories flooded my mind as the Captain addressed me as Sir. We had a full tour of the submarine, and were then taken aboard a huge Catamaran and given a guided tour around the harbour, viewing the ships.

During the whole tour, I was at times quite emotional. The way in which God had purposed all of this was to me at that time quite amazing. I kept thinking of the young boy who had 'hurt' so badly, the hatred in his heart, the contempt he held within him for some, but especially for himself. The trip was a great experience in itself, but to be treated like a VIP was just too much at times. That young man some thirty years previous would never have believed this could ever happen.

Life in the balance

Taken on the occasion of my commissioning as a Sea Cadet Chaplain. My dad had a great time teasing me over this. I know that deep down he was really proud, as they kept this photo on their bedside. I would never have believed I would ever wear a uniform again.

There is a poster in my office that says this, *"Courage, you cannot discover new oceans until you have the courage to lose sight of the shore."* Knowing Jesus has been and still is the most exciting time of my life. He has taken the wreck of a life and began to put it back together again. For whatever reason, I accept the fact that the God of the way through allows the pressure. He commands the facing up and repenting, He reveals even more of His father heart to us. There will be times of revelation, understanding to an extent, enlightenment. And then it is time to move on!

Oh yes, I have lost sight of the shore many times. The Lord has stripped me of the things that I cling on to for security, and He has at times seemed ruthless as He removes from me any presumptions I may have, or preconceived ideas concerning Him that might seek to, as it were, 'contain' Him in some way. I find it amusing at times, when I have heard people that being a Christian is necessary for those who need a 'crutch' in life.

Life in the balance

My experience has been discovering a God who spends His time taking my crutches away.

I have grown to understand that I must not be held back by holding on to attitudes, or blaming situations or other people, I am committed to the way through, He will not allow me to be tested beyond my capacity to endure. 1 Cor 10:13.

I hope you are seeing afresh how our God takes no short cuts, no easy roads with Him. He will ensure we do not go wandering off, drinking from any old place. His intention is to complete the work He has begun in us, all we have to do is hold on to Him. He will take you through with Him.

As I look at how the Lord has been moving across so many nations now, one thing is clear. It seems to me that there is a desire in the hearts of many to know Him again as a Father. That obviously means learning how to once again be childlike. Some of us are so 'grown up.' There is almost derision with some who would seek to batter us down with 'theology' and find the whole idea of 'simple childlike trust' as either naïve, or childish.

Grown men and women all across our own nation have spent hours on the floor weeping, laughing, areas of their lives that had been closed for years, opening up to the Fathers touch. Sometimes, when people realise what it is going to cost, in terms of facing up, pressing on through pressure, letting go of things that have kept them in a storm position, they try to close up again, not realising that Father is taking them on to the time when a birthing will take place.

I pray that if you are reading this, and like me, you find yourself in one of the places described herein, please, do not give in. Remember He is the God of the 'way through' it is in His nature to complete all that He begins, it may seem as

Life in the balance

though you have struggled for a long time, but it will all prove to be worth it.

"Time is what I say will be,
The end of all is up to me,
But this I say, remember well,
My pictures I will never sell.
I have a place for you to be,
A home that lasts eternally,
And their I'll keep you close to me,
The artist and His gallery.
So, no more worries no more cares,
Just try to keep away from snares,
Don't listen to the devils lies,
He'll try to rob you of your prize in me,
Your homes with me,
Come to me, my masterpiece." (portrait song).

Life in the balance

Epilogue

Running away is a way, but it is not God's way. He is the God of the way through. There are always going to be aspects to life that we naturally want to 'run from.' What I have learnt, and what I continue to learn, is that running away only ever brings discouragement, disillusionment and even depression. Most counsellors agree that many of those caught in depression, do so, often because of unresolved conflicts. Running away only increases the conflict within. Victims, who on the inside burn with indignation, anger, even hatred, yet outwardly continue to try so hard to please.

There were two words in the Royal Navy that could strike fear in the hearts of many, and cause you to live with a sense of dread. I heard these words for the first time whilst on board my very first ship, HMS Fife. The words were, 'Work up and Portland.' I couldn't understand what all the fuss was about. Stories circulated the mess deck. I was told of hardened 'sea dogs' who simply cracked up during this time. Men, who could not take the pressure any longer. I heard of guys who were taken away to a mysterious Naval establishment, and medically discharged after a prolonged period of enforced treatment. It was all just stories! Sailors are notorious for 'black catting,' this is where someone tells a story, only to have someone else tell one that is far worst.

Work up was a time where a ship and its crew spent several weeks at Portland, being brought to an 'Operational state of readiness.' In effect, you were being made ready for any, or all, of the things an RN ship could be expected to encounter. A team of men from FOST (flag officer sea training), sometimes known as 'sea riders' were on board, and were allowed to initiate literally anything. They had other names as well, (but I choose not to remember them). Their black berries and

Life in the balance

woollen jerseys identified them. All members of the crew were monitored and tested, from the Captain downwards. Looking back, I am surprised they didn't have horns and spiky tails, (maybe that's what the berries were for).

All kinds of things happened. Major fire exercises, disasters, nuclear, biological, and chemical defence (NBCD), divers trying to plant limpet mines, spies, trying to gain access to sensitive compartments. Long hours would be spent at sea testing every device on board to the limit. One in two watch keeping, no leave at all, no time off, either you were on duty, or in your bunk snatching a few hours sleep.

Food was limited to what was called 'pot mess.' Drink was limited to 'Limers.' Pot mess was exactly that, whatever the cooks had to hand went into the pot, accompanied by mashed potatoes and or cabbage. Limers, was a lime drink containing necessary vitamins.

No matter where you were or what you did there always seemed to be someone watching, assessing, taking notes, criticising and sometimes challenging, the pressure never seemed to stop for a moment.

Now another thing Sailors are good at is moaning and complaining. Every mess deck had what was called a 'mess-deck lawyer.' We were no exception, ours was called Charlie. He would regularly expound on what was allowable, and how we could exercise our rights by refusing to do that which could be considered totally unreasonable. That was until he had to unreasonably patrol the harbour wall for twelve hours looking for spies. He had an unloaded SLR (Self loading rifle), it was pouring with rain, he had no shelter, and it would be fair to say, no idea what he would do if confronted by a Royal Marine (trained killers), and challenged. Maybe Charlie would

Life in the balance

give one of his expositions on unreasonable expectations; somehow, I doubt they would have been at all effective.

Work up culminated with some intensive sea trials, followed by a few days clean ship, and finally the final inspection. This was carried out by a Rear Admiral, with a contingency of 'smary' looking officers who followed him around taking notes and agreeing with everything he said.

We were all mustered onto the flight deck to receive our expected pep talk; this usually consisted of how vital the Royal Navy was to protecting our sea-lanes. That we also played a vital role in NATO (North Atlantic Treaty Organisation), that we should be proud of the fact that we were part of a highly trained, envied by the world, elite fighting force.

Actually, we were crushed. After all we had been through, the long hours, endless tension, the mind-boggling scenario's, we were, understandably, all looking forward to a few nights leave, to bless Portland with our hard-earned cash. The rear Admiral stepped up onto the podium. The skipper had a forlorn expression, as did many of the heads of departments, what could be wrong? We were soon to discover the dreadful, unforgivable charge that was now to be levied against us. Yes, it was clear to see, the evidence was damming, we could not defend ourselves for, in his whole inspection of this huge Guided Missile Destroyer the Rear Admiral had managed to get a fine smudge on the white gloves he was wearing. He announced to us all in an accusatory tone, *"This ship is dirty!"*

The charge had been made, the sentence was pronounced. We would be required to repeat the final two weeks of workup, which was actually the worst part of it all. After the Admiral and his 'party' had left, the skipper got up to the podium. His face was one of utter dismay, he was personally hurt and

Life in the balance

offended and we had obviously let him down in a big way. He made it clear that in his opinion we had been doing so well, and we had to go and blow it all through our obvious slacking off in the last few days. The skipper went off to his day cabin, and now the 'Jimmy' (first lieutenant) got up to address us all. His was, strangely enough on this occasion, the job to play the good guy. After an excellent speech of his confidence in us to do a better job next time, he concluded with a, *"Heads up lads, lets show these !*?!*? (Naval term for 'sea-riders') what we can do, let's do it for the skipper."* Henry V would have been proud of such a speech.

Well, there was no escaping this. As unfair as it seemed to us all, this was going to happen. No appeal, no complaining could change what was now, firmly decided. It was a situation where theoretically they could keep you there until you had fulfilled the necessary requirement, that being, a white glove at the end of the inspection.

You know, it is amazing what you can discover within when you are finally placed in a position where you can no longer wriggle your way out. As I am writing this epilogue Sheila and I are on a weeks holiday in Rhodes. We have just rung home to discover our daughter in law collapsed during the Sunday morning service. She has been rushed into hospital, put on drips, and awaits the results of various tests. Literally five minutes later another member of the Church collapsed with a suspected heart attack. Returning home found Sheila's car vandalised with spray paint.

I guess we could complain, but about what? These are defining moments. We decided to Praise the Lord, for by doing that we take ourselves out of the victim mentality where life just happens to you, and like on work up, you just have to put up with it. We could enter an existence where we complain, *"why, every time we go on holiday?"* But there is another way

Life in the balance

we can go which not only takes us through, but also ensures we come through with our testimony still intact, and in victory.

One of the meanings for Praise is 'exomologeo' meaning, I will confess! So, we are defined to a degree by what we confess about our Father God. He is a good, faithful, righteous God, all of His ways are just. We can confess that when our circumstances are favourable, but do we when they are not so? We have discovered that it is also a test for those around you, the temptation for them at times to want to be a little like Job's comforters. There is a danger in trying to theologise people as they pass through different circumstances. "Why is this man blind Lord, did his parents sin?"

God's ways are higher than ours, as are His thoughts. Yet in it all, through it all, He is able to reveal to us principles that can 'keep' us on course, through the storm, or the wilderness, or the fires of refining and testing. He only requires that we trust Him with a childlike faith, and allow whatever our circumstances are, to better us, not embitter us. Whenever I have chosen to praise, faith is released. Praise is not trying to confess something bad is not happening. Praise is choosing, despite bad, negative circumstances, to deliberately confess Gods character, **nothing changes Him.** As faith is released we are enabled to face whatever lays before us in the surety and certainty of our Fathers character and strength being released through us. After the lightning strike on our home, my first sermon was entitled, "Pyrotechnical Praise."

You know, we came through with flying colours as we awaited the Rear Admirals verdict on conclusion of our second clean ship. In facing that moment together, as a crew, I actually started to believe the RN's motto, *"the team works."* And we also got our pep talk.

Life in the balance

I have no idea where you are at personally, my hope and prayer is that on reading this you will be encouraged to seek to discover the God of the way through. That means no longer running, hiding, living in denial, putting up defences, living in fear, trying to find ways round, over or back. I hope you will find a Barnabas or two, they are there, sometimes unnoticed until you need them, oft' times taken for granted. Do not fear being vulnerable, you're not half as ugly as you think you are in those moments. Actually, strangely enough I have discovered in being vulnerable others are often attracted to you.

There is no doubt in my own heart of the need to be insulated rather than isolated. We are created for fellowship, firstly with God, and also with one another. Give yourself time, my mistake has been allowing unresolved conflicts to exist within me, and at times to runaway when facing up would have brought me one step nearer to wholeness.

Weigh up the way through! Count the cost! And determine to go all the way, for every journey God undertakes is always completed.

Big boy's do cry!

A quote from Bert Crabb two weeks after becoming a Christian, *"I'm fed up with this Christianity lark, I've never cried so much in all my life."* He never did stop crying, it didn't take dad very long, just get him talking about Jesus and the tears would soon come. I am so thankful to God that I am rediscovering my tears, tears that express a simple desire, just to know Him more. Whatever the path, wherever it leads, even as the road narrows and becomes harder to travel upon, and should it mean that my life is disturbed, shaken, my dignity lay in tatters around my feet, I know it will all be worth it....

Life in the balance

A Shepherds Song *(dedicated to fellow under shepherds)*

Sometimes it's hard to see, what I am meant to be,
When shadows plague my mind, I know it's then I find,
My need for healing grace, my need to seek your face,
To feel your warm embrace, I know I've found the place.

When I can take my stand, reach out and take your hand,
And know the certainty, of love poured out for me,
Around this table Lord, your body and your blood,
They purify my soul, they leave me standing whole.

Oh precious Lamb of God, I hold aloft this rod,
That you have given me, despite this ignomy,
I bring my ugliness, and see your loveliness,
And marvel that I share, a table of such fare.

Sometimes I wonder why, I take so long to die,
This responsibility.....sometimes too much for me,
My heart is so weighed down, I'm crushed, afraid I'll drown,
What keeps my sanity....are hands that bled for me.

And so I take my place, around this table of Grace,
Despite the ones that wait, to learn about my fate,
I know my heart is well, I know that you can tell,
My heart is knit with yours, and with your body Lord.

The Church must learn to be, a place of Unity,
And then the world will see, a bride of purity,
I cast this golden crown, and fall down to the ground,
And wonder at the King, who took this cripple in.

(I wrote this song whilst preaching about Mephibosheth who ate at the Kings table).

Life in the balance

Where are we now?

Since the writing of this book back in 2000 much has happened in our lives which you can catch up on in the book entitled, 'The Roaring Forties.' We pastored a second church in Croydon and in 2015 returned to Rugby, retired from Church leadership. Sheila is a registered and accredited therapeutic counsellor working from home. I am now the Deputy Centre Manager at a Teen Challenge rehabilitation unit called Willoughby House.

We now have seven grandchildren which we thank God for. I am 65 in two-weeks time, a milestone I wasn't certain I'd ever reach. Our lives did not turn out exactly as we anticipated them to, however, we have continued to be surprised by the God who does not always act immediately, but most certainly acts suddenly.

Other books available on Amazon.co.uk

TRUST Recovery – Finding paths to freedom.
In The Wake – An accompaniment to TRUST.
The Dark Side – A journey of discovery in the area of pastoral visitation.
The Roaring Forties – Dealing with transitions in life.

Printed in Great Britain
by Amazon